On Iniquity

Books by Pamela Hansford Johnson

NOVELS

CORK STREET, NEXT TO THE HATTER'S

NIGHT AND SILENCE WHO IS HERE?

AN ERROR OF JUDGMENT

THE HUMBLER CREATION

THE UNSPEAKABLE SKIPTON

THE SEA AND THE WEDDING

CORINTH HOUSE

NONFICTION

ON INIQUITY

THE ART OF THOMAS WOLFE

ON INIQUITY

Some personal reflections arising out of
the Moors Murder Trial by Pamela
Hansford Johnson

CHARLES SCRIBNER'S SONS, New York

TO MY DAUGHTER,
Lindsay Stewart,
who said to me:
*"Don't ask what does people harm.
Ask what does them good."*

Author's Note

I was asked by *The Sunday Telegraph* to spend a day or so at the Moors Trial and write of my impressions. I intended to do no more than that. But the effect of the trial upon me was so profound, and my afterthoughts so nagging, that I felt a subsequent need to write at some length about the social implications I believed to exist, and to try to explore whether there was not, in our increasingly permissive society, some compost-heap of rottenness out of which such ugly weeds could flourish and grow lush.

The theme of this book is simple. By taking the Moors Case as a touchstone of what can go hideously wrong with two people, I am attempting to suggest that we need to do some serious re-thinking concerning several ideas perhaps thoughtlessly held to be Jeffersonian truths. I have also suggested that we all too readily comfort ourselves by believing there can be no such thing as wickedness: that there is only "sickness"—that is, a thing for which the subject bears no responsibility. I believe that some of us are, or can be, pretty wicked: and I have tried to examine whether there are things which may encourage us in wickedness, or else break down those proper inhibitions which have hitherto kept the tendency to it under restraint. The reader will note, I hope, that though obviously I have my own explicit ideas about various aspects of the dissemination of mass media which may be socially dangerous, I have done my best to avoid generalized dogmatism. I am, as I have said in Chapter 15, not answering questions, but asking them.

P.H.J.

Contents

Introduction

This is not a history of the trial; that will be written by professional criminologists in due course. But since there must be many people who either refused to read the press reports or have by now forgotten the full story, I shall set that story out briefly now.

When the trial opened in the Assize Court at Chester, on Tuesday, April 19, 1966, Ian Brady, aged 27, a store clerk, and Esther Myra Hindley, aged 23, a shorthand-typist, pleaded Not Guilty to charges that on or about October 7, 1965, in the County of Chester, they murdered Edward Evans, aged 17, of Addison Street, Ardwick, Manchester.

They both pleaded Not Guilty to charges that on a day unknown, between December 26, 1964, and October 7, 1965, they murdered Lesley Ann Downey, aged 10, of Charnley Walk, Ancoats, Manchester,* and that on a day unknown between November 23, 1963, and October 7,

* The precise day, Boxing Day, 1964, emerged in the course of the trial.

1965, they murdered John Kilbride, aged 12, of Smallshaw Lane, Ashton-under-Lyne.

Hindley alone was charged that, knowing Brady had murdered John Kilbride, she "did receive, comfort, harbor and maintain Brady." She pleaded Not Guilty.

The judge was Mr. Justice Atkinson. Sir Elwyn Jones, Q.C., the attorney-general, led for the prosecution, assisted by Mr. William Mars-Jones, Q.C., and Mr. Ronald Waterhouse.

Mr. Emlyn Hooson, Q.C., assisted by Mr. D. T. Lloyd Jones, led for the defense of Brady.

Hindley was defended by Mr. Godfrey Heilpern, Q.C., and Mr. Philip Curtis.

All the jurors were male, four women having been rejected. My husband said to me, "Perhaps a poor comment on the views held by the defense about the sensibilities of men." Yet I think myself, somewhat against my own principles, that three weeks of the horror ahead might have been a greater strain than a great many women could have contemplated.

The disappearance of John Kilbride in 1963 and of Lesley Ann Downey in 1964 had led to extensive police enquiries, continuing for weeks and months, with wide cooperation from press and public. But no trace of the children had been found.

Then, at 6:10 A.M. on Thursday, October 7, 1965, a telephone call from a kiosk unlocked the secret of the deaths and led to the investigation that solved the mystery and brought the two accused to the dock.

The call was made from Hattersley, a joyless overspill housing estate near Hyde, on the Lancashire side of the county, by David Smith, aged 17. With him was his wife

Maureen, aged 19: she was Myra Hindley's sister, but by no means so mentally bright.

The police arrived at 16 Wardle Brook Avenue, Hattersley, where Brady and Hindley lived, together with Hindley's grandmother, Mrs. Maybury, aged 77. They first surrounded the house "at a discreet and prudent distance."

There was bravery here. Superintendent Talbot borrowed, from a bread roundsman, a white coat and a basket. He went to the back door and knocked: Hindley opened. Both she and Brady were known to possess guns and to have practiced with them. The superintendent could not possibly have known what would greet him.

Hindley, told that he was a police officer, tried to stop him entering, but enter he did. When he went in, he found in Hindley's upstairs bedroom the body of Edward Evans, aged 17, bundled up and packaged in a dark-colored blanket. He had been battered to death by fourteen blows with an axe. To make assurance doubly sure, Brady had put an electric-light cable round his neck and pulled it tight.

Now, ever since the marriage of the Smiths a year before, Brady had systematically tried to deprave David, a youth already with a grubby record of violence, ten years younger than he. The couples had been much together, either in their respective houses or on bizarre wine-drinking parties in the mini-van that Hindley drove up upon the moors. Sometimes they would talk and drink into the small hours, and there must have been a great deal of talk about the books, over fifty volumes of sado-masochism, titillative pornography, torture and Nazism, which last Brady and Hindley so much admired. There was, of course, a copy of *Mein Kampf*.

The Marquis de Sade was the major hero: they had been putting some of his ideas into practice, as the digging police were to find out with their spades.

There is little doubt that Brady and Hindley were planning to translate the heated, sweating fantasies into action for Smith's benefit. They had already concocted a cock-and-bull story about robbing a bank, and being prepared to "kill if necessary." But Brady was preparing to kill in a very different fashion, to set up a murder in his house for Smith to witness.

He had said to the boy earlier, "I have killed three or four. I will do another one, but I am not due for one for another three months, but it will be done, and it won't count." (Like many of Brady's utterances, this has a gnomic ring.) Did Smith believe all this was hot air? In the event, he found it wasn't.

At 11:30 P.M. on the night of October seventh, Myra Hindley came to the Smiths' house, saying she had a message for her mother, who lived with the young couple. She then asked Smith to walk her home, since she was afraid the street lights might be turned out. He agreed to do this, and brought his stick with him.

According to his own story, he was standing in the kitchen when, "All of a sudden I heard a very loud scream, very loud. . . . Just before it died out another one followed it. Then Myra shouted out, 'Dave, help him!' I didn't know what was coming. I just ran out of the kitchen and into the living room on the left and I just froze and stopped dead. My first thought was that Ian had hold of a life-size rag doll and was just waving it about. Then it dawned on me that it was not a rag doll."

Hindley, Brady and Smith had to get busy, swabbing the blood from walls and floor, after which the young men sat down to write out a neat plan for the disposal of the body. As one of the detectives on the case told me, "Brady was the type who couldn't go on a picnic without putting it all down on paper first."

Smith then helped Brady carry the body upstairs. Brady was facetious, lightening the atmosphere with the peculiar turn of his wit. "He's a bleeder, isn't he?" "He's a dead weight." "Isn't he a *brainy* swine?" Sick jokes. Very sick.

Smith managed to get away at last, and went home to his wife. But now something went wrong, something Brady had never anticipated. Smith just couldn't take it. For one thing, the sight of so much blood turned his stomach. After an attempt to sleep, he got up and vomited. He and his young wife talked for the rest of the night. At six o'clock, they went to a telephone kiosk and called the police. Here his former record was not unhelpful. If he might hesitate to describe them as old friends, at least he knew them, and they knew him.

So it was that the secret of the moors, and of two lost children, came to light. Two other lost children remain undiscovered. Smith, with his juvenile police record of violence and his fascination with depravity, is not an endearing figure. Yet, but for the squeamishness of David Smith (whatever one may think of him), there might have been more bodies on Saddleworth Moor: never found. A policeman on the case said to me cynically, "Smith? I'm not sure he oughtn't to have a medal."

On Boxing Day, 1964, Hindley took her grandmother over to visit her uncle. When she returned there, later that evening, she told him she could not drive the old lady back: the roads were too bad, she wouldn't even attempt it—even if her grandmother had to sleep on the floor, which in fact she did. Hindley and Brady were, of course, planning to have the house to themselves.

For on that same day, Lesley Ann Downey had been enticed to Number 16, brought there by a man, or men, in a van. She was stripped, gagged, photographed in pornographic poses and then murdered. Hindley and Brady buried her naked on the moors, just as they had buried earlier the boy John Kilbride.

It was suggested by the attorney-general, in connection with both child-killings, that, "There was present not only a sexual element, but an abnormal sexual element." Not much more was made of this at the trial, except for one question, to Brady:

"Both were subjected to some kind of sexual activity before they died?"

"I don't know."

"You know that, too?"

"I don't know."

During the tormenting of Lesley Ann Downey, a very pretty little girl, small for her age, Hindley and Brady took a tape-recording of her screams and pleas for mercy, fancifully concluding the performance with seasonal music— "Jolly Old Saint Nicholas" and "Little Drummer Boy." The tape was played in the open court. It lasted over sixteen minutes. I was not present, but case-hardened crime reporters have told me that to hear it was one of the most frightful experiences of their lives. They had heard murder in progress. I have, however, read the full transcript of that tape, which was published only in *The Manchester Evening News.*

There is not much doubt that the child was submitted to gross sexual indignities after the photographs were taken and, presumably, between the two periods when she seems to have been gagged. The transcript may be read in more than one way, but only one of them really makes some dreadful sense.

The actual cause of her death cannot be determined but, since she had been gagged with a handkerchief and a scarf, probably she died of suffocation. They could have put a pillow over her face.

Brady was an enthusiastic though extremely indifferent photographer, and in the end it was lucky for justice that he was. It was his pleasure to photograph Hindley on the moors, crouching down with her dog in her arms and gazing at a disturbed patch of earth. She was, in fact, staring like a pointer at the grave of John Kilbride.

These moors seem peculiarly desolate, like acres of rubble, or a fairground after closing time, strewn with the litter of the day, the ice-cream cartons, the torn and crumpled newspapers. It was this pointless photograph, pointless because there was no obvious value in pose or location, that weighed like a slab of concrete against any hope of an acquittal on the charge of killing the little boy.

Quite early in the case, Brady admitted the murder of Evans. To the other charges, he and Hindley both pleaded that Lesley Ann had left the house safely after the photographing—"though she was tense"—and that about John Kilbride, despite the fact that his name had been found in Brady's notebook, they knew nothing at all.

The jury were out for two hours and twenty-two minutes. The accused were found guilty on all three counts, and given three concurrent sentences of life imprisonment, three for Brady and two for Hindley, plus seven years in her case, for "receiving, comforting, harboring." The judge, in passing life sentences, was brief, showing in this the moral taste he had shown throughout the trial.

They disappeared into the pit.

The bare outlines of this case are bad enough. But there is more to know, not only of the facts, but of the forces that had turned this young man and woman into what one could only conceive of as monsters.

On Iniquity

1 - *What They Were Like*

The all-permissive, the "swinging society": under its Big Top, the whole garish circus of the new freedom, freedom to revel—through all kinds of mass media—in violence, in pornography, in sado-masochism. The walls of the police storerooms are almost bulging outwards with the pressure of tons upon tons of dirty books—the ones still within the scope of the law. But there are plenty outside its scope, so we do not seem to be worrying about that just yet.

It is quite difficult, in England, to ask some simple question about the whole thing, such as, "Is what we are doing socially harmful? Because of it, do some people get hurt?" and get a sober answer. Such a question not infrequently prompts unthinking tantrums, the tantrums of a child clutching to its breast some precious, grubby toy rabbit it cannot bear to part with.

Modern criminologists such as Hermann Mannheim, psychiatrists such as Franco Ferracuti, are rejecting the theory of the "catharsis," the "safety valve." Professor Ferracuti, speaking to the American Orthopsychiatric Association in 1964, said, "It seems that portrayed violence is not

25

as innocuous, or even beneficial, as the proponents of the catharsis hypothesis maintained." This is the newest thinking: but we, as a society, appear still to be clinging to the old; we don't seem to mind who gets hurt, or even bring ourselves to consider the possibility that somebody might.

We are in danger of creating an Affectless Society, in which nobody cares for anyone but himself, or for anything but instant self-gratification. We demand sex without love, violence for "kicks." We are encouraging the blunting of sensibility: and this, let us remember, was not the way to an Earthly Paradise, but the way to Auschwitz.

When the Nazis took on the government of Poland, they flooded the Polish bookstalls with pornography. This is a fact. Why did they do so? They did so on the theory that to make the individual conscious only of the need for personal sensation would make the social combination of forces more difficult. The more we withdraw into the shell of self, breeding like tapeworms upon self alone, the less likely we are to face the problems that do not directly relate to ourselves. The Nazi scheme was the deliberate use of pornography to the ends of social castration. The theory was, and it is worth considering, that—permit all things for self-gratification, and you are likely to encourage withdrawal from any sort of corporate responsibility.

It seemed to some of us in England, that April, that we were seeing one of the results of total permissiveness in a rather comely young man and woman, ill-educated but neither of them stupid, on trial for multiple murder at Chester Assizes. A wound in the flesh of our society had cracked open, we looked into it, and we smelled its sepsis.

Chester deserved a better fate

I arrived there, on a day which had turned from un-
natural heat to grey chilliness with a threat of rain, on the
twelfth day of the trial. As it happened, my train was an
hour and a half late, so I was unable to see that night the
journalist whose lot it was to act as my bear-leader. After a
lonely dinner, I went to inspect the town, which I had
never seen before.

It is one of the most beautiful cities in England, the
only one with its Roman walls intact. Within these walls
are fine, half-timbered buildings, some leaning forward, as
if the centuries have made them feel a little giddy. The
"Rows," a double gallery of shops, the upper level ap-
proached from the pavement by stone stairways, are handy
for strolling lovers or for getting out of the rain, and at
night they glitter like the arcades in Turin.

Yet there seemed to be a sort of infective madness in
the air. I climbed the narrow, dank stairs to the ramparts
and walked some way around the town. A light drizzle was
falling now, bats were flitting in the russet-colored dusk.
As I came to a bend in the walls, I saw a couple closely em-
braced against the sweating stones. Thinking it would be
rough on them if I intruded, I began to walk back the way
I had come. Almost at once, they unlocked themselves and
began to walk in my direction. As they passed by me, I saw
that both were men.

Then I strolled in the more populated Rows, but had
not gone far when I realized that I was being dogged by an
elderly man, wearing an old mackintosh and a flat cloth
cap of some gingery material, whose aim was to keep as
close as he could to my heels, whispering dirt into my ears.
I wasn't, of course, in any danger from this obsessed old
person, yet when I found how hard it was to throw him off,
I felt my flesh creep. He spoiled my walk. I had to retreat

to my hotel: and even there, he parted from me only on the doorstep.

I am writing about these trivial experiences not because I have any hostile feeling towards the lovers on the walls or, indeed, much feeling, beyond that of irritation, about the aged whisperer. But it all seemed, in a way, indicative of the unrest, the fever, in the air. This harmless city had been forced to contain a horror: and I met nobody unaware that this was so.

Chester is a rich town, with a racecourse. The Queen had just paid a visit to the Race Week, and Chester naturally preferred to keep its eyes upon her than upon what was happening in the Assize Court in the castle on the hill.

In the bar of the hotel, comforted by brightness and noise, I began to make some notes. A woman in a rose-petal hat got into conversation with me. "I saw you were writing away like anything. I've been to the races, I didn't like the Queen's clothes at all. She was wearing emerald, or you could have called it jade. It didn't suit her. Have you come for the trial?" Yes, I said, and waited for the dread-stricken, fascination-stricken, *"What are they like?"* But no. "I haven't read any of it," she said. "I can't bring myself to and I won't." Her shudder was real.

The mass of the public had, of course, been reading the Moors Case with avidity, but there was, and it is not without significance, a sizeable minority who refused to open their minds either to the facts or to the implications of this crime. I'm not blaming them.

Apart from what they were wearing, it would have been hard to distinguish, in the hotel crowd, the race-goers from the journalists. Both seemed excited, pepped-up. The pressmen, who had been supping with horror all day, felt the relief of getting out of *"that place."* They talked compulsively about the trial, because it was the only way of squeezing some of its abomination from their systems: they could not really bear to be alone. "I like being where the lights are," said one of them, "after all that."

Yet the Assize Court itself is oddly reassuring. It is clean, bright, has been newly decorated. Canopy and curtains of red velvet, braided with gold, frame the judge's seat. The benches of the public auditorium and of the Distinguished Visitors' Gallery are upholstered in scarlet leather. Above the galleries are royal portraits: Charles II, crowned, sits with silk legs akimbo. It is a bizarre place to contain such monstrosity, even though the dock has been shut in, on three sides, with splinter-proof glass.

Well, now: what are they like?

Let us look at the accused. Ian Brady's appearance would seem to call for some reassessment of Cesare Lombroso (1836–1909), whose theories concerning biological analyses of criminal behavior have been under almost continuous attack since the time of formulation.

> The *habitual homicides* have cold, glassy eyes, immobile and sometimes sanguine and inflamed: the nose, always large, is frequently aquiline, or, rather, hooked; the jaws are strong, the cheekbones large, the hair curly, dark and abundant; the beard is frequently thin, the canine teeth well-developed and the lips delicate; frequent nystagmus and unilateral facial contraction, with a baring of the teeth and a contraction of the jaws. . . .

Brady is much taller than he seems. He is probably short-bodied, for when he sat beside Hindley in the dock, he seemed shorter than she. He is very thin, small-shouldered, his chest concave. His face is almost tragically gaunt. The bones of the large, beaked nose, of the cheeks, of the strong, if narrow, jaw seem to shine through the flesh. If he shows emotion at all, it is in the contraction of the cheek-muscles, the tightening of the well-cut mouth.

He is a cross between Joseph Goebbels and a bird. His hair is median brown, thick, wavy, lying back from his forehead like plumage; his entire coloring seems to be in various tones of that brown, which gives him a monochrome appearance. His eyes are cold and pale. He is dressed in a grey suit, a white handkerchief natty in his breast-pocket. On the whole, he looks ordinary.

Myra Hindley does not. Sturdy in build and broad-buttocked, though her face, hands and feet appear to be narrow and delicate, she could have served a nineteenth-century academy painter as a model for Clytemnestra; but sometimes she looks more terrible, like one of Fuseli's nightmare women drawn giant-size, elaborately coiffed, with curled and plaited maidservants reaching no higher than her knee. She wears a grey, double-breasted suit with six buttons, a sky-blue shirt open at the neck, the cuffs neatly drawn down below the sleeves of her jacket. She was dark, once; now she is a Nordic blonde. Her hair is styled into a huge puffball, with a fringe across her brows. At the beginning of the trial it was rinsed to a lilac shade, now it is melon-yellow. The style is far too massive for the wedge-shaped face; in itself, it bears an uneasy suggestion of fetichism. But it is the lines of this porcelained face which are extraordinary. Brows, eyes, mouth are all quite straight, precisely parallel. The fine nose is straight, too, except for a very faint downward turn at the tip, just as the chin turns very faintly upward. She will have a nutcracker face, one day.

How would she look if her hair were not dyed, if her

face were unpainted? It is only fair to ask that question. Would she seem as ordinary as Brady, someone easy to pass by upon the street? Now, in the dock, she has great strangeness, and the kind of authority one might expect to find in a woman guard of a concentration camp.

In the witness-box, both were controlled and quiet: steadily and remorselessly, sometimes ingeniously, sometimes crassly, they lied and lied. Yet there was not always this quietude. Brady was twice in the box while the jury retired, since a legal submission was being debated. I was not there at the time, but I am told that he displayed a ferocity and arrogance terrifying in its intensity. Once he rounded upon the attorney-general with dirty language that spouted from him like oil from a well. He must have been cautioned by his own counsel not to repeat this performance when the jury came back into court.

He has a glottal Scots accent.

What were they both thinking? It is almost impossible to imagine. "Evil, be thou my good?" Or: "But this is *us*. You have no right to pass judgment upon us."

Novelists are conceited people; they tend to believe there is no mind into which they cannot imagine themselves, and here Dostoevski may have misled almost all writers who have tried to penetrate into the criminal consciousness. He has such demonic projective force that we tend to swallow whatever he tells us. He believes in the ultimate triumph of repentance in the murderer, that he *must* come to hate what he has done. He has given us Raskolnikov as a prototype. Yet the killer for gain or for personal gratification is almost always lacking in what the psychologists call *affect*—that is, any capacity for entering into the feelings of others. I believe very few of the guards in the concentration camps were true sadists: what had disappeared in them was the capacity to think of those they tortured as human beings at all. The prisoners were animals; they didn't have the same feelings as ourselves. There have been far more horrors committed in our time by the affectless than by the pathologically cruel.

We are living in a society which continuously encourages affectlessness, and we see its effects all round us; from the mobs who break into a children's playground and insert pieces of jagged glass through the planks in the slide, from the gangs who will beat up innocent people for "kicks" (that depraved word we have all lightly accepted), to the couple who buried Lesley Ann Downey and John Kilbride, making the moors an Abomination of Desolation in all the dreadful reality of that phrase.

In this courtroom I learned a hard lesson: empathy in this case was impossible. I made a conscious effort to feel pity, but could do so for the flesh alone; the fatigue of the bone, the fallen cheek, the scoops of darkness under the eyes, the visible ravages of fear and hate. But one cannot imagine oneself into the situation of these two, far less into their heads. One cannot hear the tape-recorder that Brady carries in his skull: of this we shall never read the transcript.

It shook me that this was so, that I could not feel pity: but it would be sentimentalism if I pretended that I did. For this was something out of the human scale as we conceive it, even out of the common scale of murder. False empathy, in such circumstances, would have been dangerous simply because of its falsity.

Compassion is the greatest of the virtues, yet the mere word has been so debased that it may be used to cover a multitude of sentimentalities. There are times in this life when we *cannot* feel it, and are so alarmed because we cannot that we tend to cook up a story, to make us appear better people and richer in human insight.

What I felt in Hindley's presence was terror. I asked others, pressmen, policemen, how they felt. They felt as I did, without a single exception.

As one detective said to me, *"You* were terrified? *I* was terrified!" He told me that in the prison where she was being held on remand, officers would take turns to go to her with meals, or on any other errand. "No, I went last time. It's your turn now." This was, of course, not a physical but a spiritual fear.

It was, however, possible to grasp that, dominant as Hindley might appear, she was not Lady Macbeth. She had no previous police record. She was once a Roman Catholic —indeed, a left luggage-ticket brought into evidence was discovered in the spine of the prayer book given her on the occasion of her First Communion. She was a baby-sitter much sought after by mothers. Her mind seems to have been bigoted in the crudest sense: she would talk of "dirty niggers," "filthy coloreds."

Then she came under the thumb of Brady and was consistently depraved by him. Now she seems to carry the burden of this depravity almost contemptuously, except for her few admissions of shame at the sight of the photographs, her admissions that yes, she was cruel to Lesley Ann.

"Yes, I was cruel."

"And pitiless?"

"I was cruel."

The word "pitiless" she refused to admit.

She appeared to be devoted to Brady who, during her

evidence, did not once look at her. "I loved him . . . I love him still." "If he asked me to do something . . . I always went along with him eventually." It is probable that once she was not nearly so strong as he, though she has become so now.

When her grandmother, hearing the screams of Evans, asked what all the noise was about, Hindley shut her up promptly. "I told her it was the dogs barking."

I heard the owl scream and the crickets cry.

Still, she was no Lady Macbeth.

Each of the accused made some attempt to exculpate the other. Yet there is something baffling in this relationship. Was Brady homosexual? Bisexual? Women have been desperately in love with such men before, appetite growing not by what it feeds on, but by what it is denied. Was any sexual assault made by Brady on Evans? A dog's hairs, found on the *inside* of his clothing, indicate that at some time or another that evening, Evans was naked. He seems to have been an invert; it was to him that Brady was referring when he spoke of planning to "roll a queer" (rob a homosexual). But was a sexual assault made on John Kilbride and, if so, did Hindley know it?

When the police, with understandable reluctance, took the clothes of the long-buried boy from their plastic containers, a stench of corruption rose which filled the entire courtroom. One man whispered, "It takes me back to the trenches of Flanders in 1916." A French reporter said, "My God, have the English got no noses?"

Over the whole of this trial, and behind it, there was a psychic stench. There had been persistent rumors of the involvement of far more people than two in the hideous amusements enjoyed by Hindley and Brady, but I think these may be discounted. Certainly the police discount them, and they are as eager as all of us to see a total cleansing.

But nevertheless, during these hours in court, most of us felt we were seeing only the eighth of the iceberg.

2 - A Book List

Not so long ago, I raised a little storm by suggesting, in a letter to *The Guardian,* that it was not desirable for Krafft-Ebing to be available in relatively cheap paperback on the bookstalls of English railway stations.

Was I, then, taking a stand against the totally permissive and promulgating that all works should not be available to all people? To this I reply, unequivocally: that is what I was suggesting. There are some books that are not fit for all people and some people who are not fit for all books.

Before I am assailed by libertarian outcries, let me elaborate my point.

The *Psychopathia Sexualis* is an important work which was written for experts in the field of sexology. If it is to be read scientifically and not destorted by being scooped up as a work of sexual titillation, accompanied by "Oohs" and "Aahs," then it demands that the reader shall have made some previous study of the subject and can take the *Psychopathia* as both synthesis and extension of what he already knows. An ill-educated reader in search of excitation is likely to get from it only some new and interesting ideas that may provoke him to introspection of a non-illuminating nature, to fantasticating onanism, or, at worst, to the concept of putting some of the ideas into practice. The fact is that we are offering at random those full liberties which would only be justifiable if offered to a far more highly educated people than we are. It might be urged that our only recourse now would be to step up our education in an attempt to bring us all into line with the present *assumption* of our scientific-mindedness—a counsel of perfection, I am afraid, and one not tenable for anybody with the slightest statistical sense. No country in the history of the world has yet educated itself to this pitch.

It is no use for us to pretend that we are an ideal society, fully mature, with free choice and rich leisure. This is what we hope to become, but now are not: when we are so, there will be no need for censorship of any kind whatsoever. But we are seeing the most fantastic growth of a semi-literate reading public—semi-literate, no more, yet, than that: and at the same time we are prepared to offer, to minds educationally and emotionally unprepared, "total publication" in almost every form of mass media. This is why we need to adjust ideal legal aims with the actual possibilities of conduct, and we cannot do this until we understand far more of what those possibilities are.

We are shouting in the dark for what we *want:* we need to turn up the lights before we can understand what we may, without endangering the structure of our society, actually have.

This is true, not only of what we are doing to the semi-educated, but to those of us who have been luckier. If I understand him correctly, such is a major theme of Dr. Philip Rieff's *The Triumph of the Therapeutic,* which is asking some of the deepest questions of our time. As it is, we have put the cart before the horse, and if the cart looks more often like a dung-cart than is comfortable, then we need to overhaul some of our fashionable shibboleths.

Let me make a debating point and hope that it may be answered. Are we to believe that all works in all medical libraries should be offered freely (and cheaply) to the public? If we did this, we should enormously increase hypochondria and the fear of death. That this new flood of literature would bring in the money, I have no doubt: but at what cost? Not a lethal one, probably; but high, nevertheless, in social terms.

I am inclined to think that it is less good to make things easy for the prurient than to make him work a little harder for his gratification. If he feels he cannot be truly happy without reading the report of the trial of Gilles de Retz (to Sade as Pitt is to Addington) he can probably find his way, with a degree of application, to the archives of the Bibliothèque Nationale. And a resolute attempt to obtain a ticket to the Reading Room of the British Museum may uncover for him much in any of his chosen fields. The mere difficulty of finding the salacity he craves might be the saving of a rather irresolute, or lazy, pornographer.

Neither David Smith nor Ian Brady had received the kind of education likely to fit them for objective study, though both Brady and Myra Hindley were of slightly more than average I.Q. Their interests were sado-masochistic, titillatory and sado-Fascist, and in the bookshops they found practically all the pabulum they needed, though one or two of their books were, I suppose, smuggled.

This library, consisting of fifty-odd books, a few of

which were harmless enough, is divided sharply into three groups. Here is a selection: but I must add that some of these works were socially and scientifically responsible in intention and not designed for study outside a specialist world.

Sado-Masochistic

THE HISTORY OF CORPORAL PUNISHMENT
THE HISTORY OF TORTURE THROUGH THE AGES
ORGIES OF TORTURE AND BRUTALITY
THE PLEASURES OF THE TORTURE CHAMBER
SEX CRIMES AND SEX CRIMINALS
DE SADE
THE LIFE AND IDEAS OF THE MARQUIS DE SADE

Titillatory

EROTICA
THE ANTI-SEX
SEXUAL ANOMALIES AND PERVERSIONS
CRADLE OF EROTICA
HIGH HEELS AND STILETTOS
KISS OF THE WHIP

Dealing with Fascism and Nazism

NUREMBERG DIARY
HEINRICH HIMMLER
MOSLEY RIGHT OR WRONG
THE MARK OF THE SWASTIKA

There was also the copy of *Mein Kampf,* and, not surprisingly in the context, two books on how to teach oneself the German language.

Brady, in the box, was huffy when questioned about

his library. The attorney-general offered him a list of the books which, he said, he did not wish to read out. He asked: "They are all squalid pornographic books?"

Brady: "They cannot be called pornography. They can be bought at any bookstall."

"They are dirty books, are they not?"

"It depends on the dirty minds."

"This was the atmosphere of your mind?"

"No."

It is interesting that this is the stereotype response of our time. Contemporary apologists could have done no better.

I cannot help but wonder whether, by making all books available to all men, we do not pay too high a price, if that price should be the death of one small child by torture. I shall have to return to this point. No one can prove a causal connection between what these two people read and what they did. It might have happened anyway. But if there were a causal connection, how does one weigh in the balance the libertarian principle of making all books available to all men, and the death of a child in such a fashion? I have no doubt how I weigh them.

(Both Hindley and Brady, by the way, refused to take the oath, and affirmed: about this they seemed more adamant, certainly more morally indignant, than about other, and ugly, matters. They had made their own rules and they abided by them.)

I do not want to overstate my case.

At the same time as the Moors Trial was proceeding, a housewife from an industrial district of Indianapolis, aged 47, sat in the dock with her two daughters, aged 17 and 15, her son aged 13, and two neighborhood boys, both aged 15. They were charged with having over the period of a fort-

night beaten, starved, branded, scalded and ultimately
murdered a pretty but obviously dim-witted girl whom the
housewife had taken into her care. It was a familiar pattern. The girl had been tied to a bed, refused water or the
use of a lavatory. When she wet the bed, she was beaten
for dirtiness. It was the old story of deciding that a fellow
creature was subhuman, and then punishing her—I suspect
with *moral indignation*—for her supposed subhumanity.

Now I do not for a moment suppose that the accused
in this trial had access to a library so diverse, or so specialized, as Brady's. Indeed, from the accounts I have read, I
should be surprised to find there was a book in the house.

Yet how much violence, of permitted depravity, had
they picked up in the air? There are very few intellectuals
indeed who will now lend themselves to serious discussion
as to whether, by mass communications of all kinds, we in
the west are not poisoning that air, whether it may be due
to its infection that some children die. In fact, any attempt
to get them to discuss the subject responsibly and without
exaggeration often drives them into a strange state of hys-
teria, of the curious kind of unreason one sometimes meets
in religious controversy, or of total silence.

The more recent Chicago murder by one man of eight
young nurses seems to me, on the available evidence, something different in kind; here a killer appears to have lured
the eight into acquiescence at being trussed up for slaugh-
ter by suggesting that he only wanted money and would
not hurt them. Apparently he induced five of the girls,
sleeping together in a dormitory, to do as he wished, his
only weapon being a large butcher's knife. There was no
evidence of threat by shooting—indeed, it would seem
dubious whether the murderer even had a gun. What is
puzzling at this stage, with due respect for the terror the

girls must have felt, was the lack of opposition to the killer. Could this present quite another problem? Could the violence in our air have persuaded these young people that the cry, "Dilly-dilly, come and be killed," is now impossible to meet by a concerted refusal to do anything of the kind? We may all be anesthetised by the air we breathe, not only into becoming murderers, but victims also. We may have been led into believing that there is nothing else for it but to put our hands up from the word "go."

The point is delicate. We have a free press, almost free dissemination in every form of mass communications: these may be the staples of our liberty.

But what is such liberty worth, without self-control by each and every one of us who profits from it?

I ask again: what is the price we are prepared to pay?

3 - The Affectless Society

"I have seen butchers working in the shops show as much emotion as he did when they are cutting up a sheep's ribs."

Thus David Smith, describing Brady at work on Edward Evans.

The attorney-general, to Brady:

"What were your feelings when striking the boy with this axe? What were your emotions?"

Answer: "I didn't have any. I can't remember what my emotions were. I was just hitting him."

The attorney-general: "I suggest to you that you were inducing this boy to think he was among friends and you got him to go to your home?"

Brady: "Yes."

"You never intended Evans to leave that living room alive?"

"Yes."

"What is more, you had a grave on the moors in mind for him, is that right?"

"That's right, after discussion."

"Before discussion?"

"No."

"Before the murder?"

"No."

"You had in mind to commit a murder that night and bury the victim where you had buried the others?"

"That night I came home and went out with the dog and took some photographs."

Later, his questioning now upon the subject of Lesley Ann Downey, the attorney-general asked Brady about the photographs of the child.

"Do you think they are horrible?"

Brady: *"Not necessarily."* (The italics are mine.)

The pictures, of which I had only a brief glimpse, were appalling.

Here is something from a different trial, reported by Sibylle Bedford.*

One night a young merchant seaman went to the Paddington flat of a homosexual, cooked his host a chicken, drank some wine and let in his mates later. They knocked their host down and tied him up. Then, enraged to find no money, they kicked and beat him to death. After taking his teeth out (a baffling detail) they laid him on the bed.

Miss Bedford goes on:

A witness says that the cool young man told him, in the prison hospital, that he had burned all his clothes and bought an identical set from the same shop. This the cool young man denies.

The judge: "Not so fast. *Wait.*"

Young man: "It was a joke."

Counsel, in cross-examination (Driving very hard): "Why did you tell this story?"

* *The Observer Colour Supplement,* May 15, 1966.

> Young man: "I dunnow . . . I was fed up. . . .
> (*Sotto voce*) A copper's nark—"
> The judge: "Listen! *Why did you tell this story?*"
> Young man: "I was pulling his leg."

What are the roots of all this affectlessness? From whence comes this peculiar and all-too-recognizable tone? I asked a reputable bookseller what he thought. He replied, "I believe it in our life today."

So do I. Or if you will not go all the way with me, let me suggest that we may be creating an atmosphere in our life, in "London, the Swinging City," as *Time* magazine has it, and in other urban centers, which may result in grave infection to our social health. In a sense Brady possibly, Hindley almost certainly, have been victims of fallout.

It is rather hard to see where it all began: probably the floodgates opened less than ten years ago. But let us try to examine a few factors in our conditioning towards the affectless state.

Well, there was the "sick" joke, at which Brady became so adept, the cruel birthday or Valentine card, designed to wound, designed to encourage the abnegation of human feeling. There was the TV "satire" program, which at first seemed conducive to a salubrious expression of protest at social ills and anomalies, but all too speedily gave an opportunity for some invented television "personality," addressing a vast audience, to wreak cruelty upon individuals. Audiences loved it: it was a restoration of the pillory, the stocks and the ducking-stool as spectator sports.

Yet some of these programs were lively, vigorous, funny and of genuine social value, such as the sketch, during the Vassall Tribunal, showing the hapless Civil Servant being warned that he could not even sign a letter "Yours faithfully" without being suspected of homosexuality. The ugliness, indeed, may have formed a small part of the whole: but ugliness there was.

Then there came the catch-phrases of excuse for anti-social behavior: "I did it for a joke." "It was a bit of a giggle." *"I was bored."*

The last is the most touted excuse of all, touted especially by hooligans who have wrecked an infant school, smashed every telephone booth in an area where somebody without a telephone of his own might desperately need a doctor or an ambulance, beaten up a middle-aged man or woman for "kicks."

"I didn't like the way he looked at me, see?"

But I have heard quite un-criminal adolescents claim, as an excuse for bad behavior, "I was bored."

The only answer to this is, "I'm sure you were. But this is not a permanent state. The great majority of us are bored, at some time or another, for some part of our lives. So why shouldn't you be?"

At about the same period, jeering about the Christian religion also became "good for a giggle"—one of the most affectless phrases of our decade. It is curious that this happened more or less at the time when libertarians were campaigning for a tightening-up of the law in respect of anti-semitism or any kind of racial hatred. Very odd. It is true that many Christians did complain at some of the more gross insults offered to their faith, but they were generally considered in the light of fuddy-duddies, if not as Ancient Druids. The symptoms, rather than the results, have social importance.

The floodgates to total permissiveness on the book-stalls were opened by the *Lady Chatterley* case. Here I do not wish to be misunderstood. (People in certain kinds of

anger, as in paranoia, lose the capacity to read.) If I had
been in England at that time, I should unquestionably have
slouched into the witness-box in its defense, though I
should not have emphasized its Puritan qualities. (John
Sparrow was quite right, though irrelevant.) I think it is
one of Lawrence's poorest books, exemplifying his lack
of any sense of the ridiculous. But if Penguin publica-
tions wished to publish the entire works of a writer of his
standing, then they were entitled to include this rather
lame duck.

The immediate result of the verdict was to make a
number of people feel the *necessity* for using four-letter
words morning, noon and night. For weeks after the trial,
I couldn't walk down Earl's Court Road without hearing
these superbities ringing out in fresh young voices, as
freaked with defiance as the pansy with jet. This spell
didn't last long: the young, sometimes more sensible than
their elders, by instinct if not by fashion, got a little bored.
But many writers feel something is lacking these days if
they do not pepper their novels with the permitted words
as American writers used to pepper them with very
strained Symbols. (If anyone takes this as a manifestation
of anti-Americanism, let me refer them to Mary McCarthy,
who feels as bleakly on the subject of symbols as I do.)

It is not Lawrence's fault. Yet it is almost axiomatic
that when anything goes, everything goes. He is not at all a
dirty writer: he is, whether you feel he is God or not, a
writer with tremendous projective force. He is also capable
of infinite silliness, and, though this is incidental, almost
inconceivable social reaction. *Lady Chatterley* had to be
released, and I should have testified to that effect: but it
would probably have been better if he hadn't written it.

Since that verdict, many writers, especially in America, have become infinitely boring. Does writing a four-letter word represent reality? If you write it often enough, it will look as interesting as "butter" or "mouse." For art is not the stuff of the tape-recorder: art is always, by its very nature, selective, and lies chiefly in the choice and arrangement of material. *Anna Karenina* is a work far more deeply imbued with the atmosphere of sexual passion than *Lady Chatterley's Lover,* though there is not, as they say, "a word out of place"; even if Tolstoi had had the liberty to spell out copulation syllable by syllable, I doubt if he would have availed himself of the privilege. To analyze, centimeter by centimeter, an experience common to the vast majority of mankind would seem to me like analyzing, as if by fashionable compulsion, the shelling and eating of a boiled egg—an experience, alas, rather less common, if we realize the gap between comfort and starvation in this world, though in western countries it is an action ordinary enough to go without comment.

If "anything goes," everything goes. The stuff loading down our railway bookstalls is to a very high extent the stuff of corruption, or is harmless stuff deliberately dressed up to look as if it were so.

Instant Fashion goes against saying this. But let us consider, for a moment, what Instant Fashion is: it is chorus-singing, it is doing, with a feeling of coziness and security, what the next man does. It is a very pleasant thing to be free of the independent voice, and to move with a crowd is a blessed insulation from the harshness of personal decision. Nevertheless, each and every one of us needs to take account, from time to time, of whether the fashion suits him. In physical terms, is his shape right for it? Are his legs long enough, is his stomach flat enough? In spiritual terms, is his mind right for it? Does he really believe in what he is saying, is his voice really in tune with the heavenly choir?

It is agreeable to be in tune with any popular song, even if it may seem to be a song of non-conformity. But it is well to remember that in any form, by its very nature, Instant Fashion is always vulgar.

4 - Seventy-five Tons

Since I am very fond of my country and have a certain fondness for the U.S.A., I do not wish to see England or America looking absurd—which, to large parts of the world, both of us unquestionably do. The Americanized Saigon must, if we listen to Senator Fulbright, be as ludicrous as degenerate. But, of course, we have our Saigons all over the British Isles. English-speaking visitors from Communist countries to our own deride us for the scrofulous appearance of our bookstalls; not only hard-shell old Stalinists, but the younger, western-oriented intellectuals. On their side, they have a price to pay, and often, even since the Stalin apparatus was broken down, it has been a shocking one. But what price must we be prepared to pay if we want to educate our children to the sense of—yes, how bizarre it sounds!—social responsibility? I do not like my country to be sneered at by the other half of the world.

At present, we are looking, in the arts, less like an up-and-coming socialist state than like the last years of the Weimar Republic.

All right: what happened after that?

Hitler.

But must we take this to mean that if we raise the slightest protest against sadistic seediness and more sadistic seediness, Hitlerism will result? If so, we have abrogated responsibility and are presenting ourselves to the world as moral eunuchs. We are behaving like cowards, and brainless cowards at that. Because solutions are difficult, we have been refusing to search for them.

Most of the reputable booksellers and almost all public librarians are seriously worried. As one of the latter said, "I don't want all this sadistic stuff on my shelves. But they come in and they demand *Justine*, and since it's permitted, I've got to get it." (I am told that the demand for this work is even greater since the Moors Case.) A commercial bookseller told me: "We watch the young people pour in and we see what they read. Even a serious work will attract them if the cover is smutty in implication. We hate every bit of it, but there's nothing much we can do."

I asked him, "Do you suppose that if they buy *Anna Karenina*, for instance, in a titillatory jacket, it eventually does them good?"

Like the carpenter, he doubted it. The result, he said, was far more likely to be outrage, and a sense of having been gypped.

Two articles appeared in successive weeks in *The Sunday Telegraph*, by Giles Playfair, and by a team of investigators into the pornographic bookshops of London and three other large towns,* both raising the question of whether it is too easy to buy the sort of books found in Brady's suitcases. Giles Playfair says the psychiatric opinion he consulted was at one in feeling that the "philoso-

* May 8, 1966; May 15, 1966.

phy" of Sade might have provided Brady with the rational-
ization he needed for murder. "It may have represented
the final conquest of his miserably weak scruples."

He continues: "None of this is proof that *Justine*
ought to be peremptorily banned. But there seems to be an
imperative call for a proper investigation into the causal
connection between gross crime and sadistic literature of a
sexually stimulating or sadistic kind, with the object of deciding what real necessity there may be for granting law
enforcement additional powers to stamp out hard-core
pornography and deliberate titillation."

The investigating team make it clear, at least, that the
police try hard enough.

> At Scotland Yard, the Obscene Publications Squad
> . . . has fourteen men who devote almost all their time
> to the pursuit and seizure of filth. Working all round the
> clock in twenty-four hours, they often make seven or
> eight raids on shops and clubs in the Metropolitan area
> alone.
>
> They have now a stock of *seventy-five tons* of obscene
> material: it has grown so much lately that they have been
> forced to take over more stores in which to accommodate
> it. Even this enormous amount represents only a small
> proportion of what they seize: they keep a consignment
> only till a court has ordered the conviction of the former
> owner, and then they burn it or send it for conversion
> into pulp.

The average dirty bookshop in the Soho area—since
Maurice Girodias, I believe, uses the term "dirty books"
quite happily I am not going to search for some mollifying
synonym—seems to operate in a tripartite fashion. First
there is the window display, showing titillative and sado-
masochistic commonplaces—*The Perfumed Garden,* the

Kama Sutra, Pleasures of the Torture Chamber and the usual "girlie" magazines. Inside, there is a room containing matter rather more extreme. American magazines, selling at £2 or £3 each, are carefully taped or sealed so that the customer will have to buy. Kid's stuff, really, by the standards of what the bookseller has in store for you in his inner room, provided he will let you go there. Here you may be permitted to "browse" for a sum ranging between five shillings an hour, or a £4 entrance fee.

"The attendant was constantly burrowing under the counter for supplies. Men came in and out steadily. Most were clearly regular customers and were greeted with remarks like, 'Hullo, guv. What's it today? Flag or straight?'" ("Flag" means flagellation.)

But, say the defenders of total permissiveness, who are we to deprive the customer of what he craves, to deny him his own form of happiness?

Many people can read pornography with no harm to society or to themselves: some people can take drugs with similar lack of effect. But it is foolish to think that, when one has said this, one has said all that need be said about either the individual or the social implications.

I shall quote almost the whole of a letter to *The Sunday Times,* by Dr. Leslie Weatherhead.*

> It is alleged that the criminals involved in the "Moors Case" had mentally absorbed the writings of the Marquis de Sade and others. Most of us have *tendencies* towards sexual perversion and cruelty, and if our reading feeds these tendencies, and subsequently some unexpected situation offers opportunity, it is possible that tendencies could become deeds followed by lifelong regret.
>
> "However could such a man have come to do such a

* May 15, 1966.

thing?" was asked when a famous person unleashed such tendencies in detected action. The answer was the literature found in his desk after he had fled the country.

Many feel that any kind of censorship is narrow-minded and an attack on liberty. Yet we do not allow people to purchase poisons or dangerous drugs without attempting to prevent them. Why should we not merely allow but advertise mental poisons—like Sade's writings, for instance—and allow floods of pornography to pollute our bookstalls and subsequently the minds of our fellows?

"What harm can we do? People must learn to know the facts of life." This is said by those who forget that a dead rat in a stinking sewer is a fact, but this is no reason for putting it on the menu.

I think that the happily married and the sexually satisfied have no idea of the mental torture of others who are stimulated by mental poisons and yet have no honourable way of finding satisfaction. . . .

To be starving in a room containing no food would be trial enough, but to be able, from such a room, to see and smell food, yet be unable to reach it, would be mental torture. To be sexually hungry is the fate of thousands, both young and old. There is nothing evil in this hunger, but it is hard to bear. To have it stimulated when it cannot be honourably satisfied is to make control more difficult.

He is no friend of society who, by mental poisons and stimulants, makes life harder for others.

This is a statement by a man of deep experience, whom no one could accuse of bigotry or of failure to "face facts." I do not recall that anyone replied to Dr. Weatherhead. There was just silence, as though he had thought the unthinkable.

(Of course, there is much nonsense about this "fact-facing." Half the people who are so keen on it mean only certain facts—that is, facts about sexual anomaly and perversion, facts of hooligan violence. There would not be such a wide interest in the written record, or staging of, the squalid and terrible facts of hunger and misery over wide areas of the world.)

The stage presents another problem. At best, the English theater is finer than it has ever been, and I think we are right to be proud of it. But certain London theaters have been putting on, again and again, displays of violence and cruelty that make my mind boggle, though other minds appear to regard them as a kind of social therapy. This is, it is argued, true catharsis: if we work out our aggressions vicariously, we shall free ourselves from the desire to put them into action and become better and kinder people. If this were so, the entire staff of publishers of pornographic books, everyone, from actors to stage-hands, connected with performances at certain London theaters, the concentration camp guards of Nazi Germany, would by this time have become the nicest and kindest people God ever made

Now we have been seeing on the stage, in the past few years, the torture of a priest, the pitchforking of an agricultural laborer, the kicking to death of an old man, and, more recently, the torment and murder of a baby in a perambulator by a gang of louts, who roll it in its own excrement and then stone it to death.*

Not everyone felt about this last work as I did. Mr. William Gaskill, Director of the Royal Court Theatre and therefore responsible for it, said this in an interview in *The Spectator* (Nov. 10, 1965):

* Laurence Kitchin's book, *Drama in the Sixties* (Faber), studies this phenomenon more closely than I am able to do here.

Have you ever seen a baby stoned to death on the stage before? Or a flabby old bag rousing sexual excitement in a young man? I think it is a triumph to have these things put on the stage.

I have to ask: why is it a triumph? Can Mr. Gaskill mean that the presentation on the stage of *anything* that has not been permitted before is in itself a triumph? If not, what on earth does he mean?

Let me sharpen my query by example. He knows, presumably, as well as I do, the details of the execution of Ravaillac, who assassinated Henry IV of France. If it were possible to reproduce those details, as nearly as possible, in a public theater, whether by tricks of stagecraft or by symbolism close enough to shock, would he consider that a triumph? If so, why? A "triumph" is a useless thing unless it is a means to an end. What end has Mr. Gaskill in mind?

But let me go further. Perhaps he has grasped the revolting details of the murder of Lesley Ann Downey. If we could reproduce those on the stage, would that be a triumph? If not, why not?

I am afraid Mr. Gaskill's triumphs are always going to be small beer in comparison with what has already happened. In the Roman theater, you could even see a real crucifixion on the stage.

The baby-stoning play, by Edward Bond, called *Saved*, caused an immediate storm of protest from nearly all the major dramatic critics, who found the now-notorious scene too sickening to endure.

I do not speak of this play lightly. I have read and re-read it with the greatest care, and remain of the opinion that the scene to which I refer is, despite its verbal skill, unfit for public representation. Either it sickens, or it con-

duces to the wrong kind of excitation. It is not conducive
to social thinking, since it contains no shock of new knowl-
edge.

I am not blind to the symbolism underlying the scene
I find so intolerable, both emotionally and socially. It is in
Blake's dictum: "Better strangle an infant in its cradle
than nurse unacted desires."

Now Blake, a glorious and a heady poet, was only mad
nor-nor-west: he can make statements (there are many in
the Prophetic Books) that seem suddenly to illuminate a
whole life like a light flashing up in one single room of a
darkened doll's house. But he can also make statements
that are, if interpreted literally (which he himself cannot
have meant should happen), merely mad: and I say this
statement is mad and wrong. (Many great statements have
been mad and right.) *It is much better to nurse unacted
desires than to strangle an infant in its cradle.* Most of us
nurse such desires our whole lives long: we must do, if we
are social animals, since if we indulged them it would be to
the danger and misery of our fellow men. If there is one
thing in this life as certain as death and taxes, it is that no
living person can have everything he wants for himself,
and the struggle to behave as if he can is as vain as the
search for Eldorado or the philosopher's stone.

It is only fair to let Mr. Bond answer his detractors—
even though a writer's explicit intentions have almost no
connection with what he has actually achieved:

> *Saved* is almost irresponsibly optimistic. Len, the
> chief character, is naturally good, in spite of his upbring-
> ing and environment, and he remains good in spite of the
> pressures of the play. But he is not wholly good or easily
> good because then his goodness would be meaningless, at
> least for himself. His faults are partly brought home to

him by the ambivalence at the death of the baby and his morbid fascination with it afterwards.

(Len, who had put himself *in loco parentis,* hid in the trees while the murder was going on, a witness too scared to intervene. I like the word "ambivalence" in this context.)

Concerning the stoning scene itself:

> In particular, the murder of the baby shows the Oedipus [*sic*], atavistic fury fully unleashed. The scene is typical of what some people do when they act without restraint, and it is not true just of these particular people and this particular occasion. Everyone knows of worse happenings. That sort of fury is what is kept under painful control by other people in the play, and that partly accounts for the corruption in their lives.

Can Mr. Bond mean that if the other characters released their violence and also murdered babies, this would *lessen* the corruption of their lives? He continues:

> Clearly the stoning to death of the baby in a London park is a typical British understatement. Compared to the "strategic" bombing of German towns it is a negligible atrocity, compared to the cultural and emotional deprivation of most of our children its consequences are insignificant.

This is inadequate thinking. The murder of one single child is made negligible by *nothing,* not even by Hiroshima. The murder of Lesley Ann Downey and John Kilbride cannot be made negligible by a hundred Hiroshimas. Mr. Bond's statement shows the common fallacy of feeling for the "masses" while minimizing the importance of feeling for individuals.

Support came to him from Sir Laurence Olivier:

Saved is not for children but it is for grown-ups, and the grown-ups of this country should have the courage to look at it. . . .

Why? In all seriousness, *why?*

Most intellectual adults will have read the Pro and Contra section of *The Brothers Karamazov*. It is preposterous to pretend people don't know that such monstrosities happen. (We have always *The News of the World* to remind us.) Are such plays as *Saved* intended to enlighten our ignorance? We are not ignorant at all. But to the great majority of people, including myself, it would be a mere exercise in sado-masochism repeatedly to witness graphic representations of the human beastliness we already know to exist. That would be really treating ourselves as children.

Now I have only used Mr. Bond's play as an example of the results of total permissiveness because it is the "farthest-out" of others in the same *genre,* and indeed I am sorry to add to his burdens. I suppose I must rather laboriously explain that by doing so I am not accusing him personally of having a part in anything that led finally to the child-killers in the dock at Chester. I am well aware that a relatively small number of people (in the total population of London) have actually seen his play—or any play. The theater remains a minority art. Mr. Bond is far more a victim of the modish atmosphere than the atmosphere is a victim of Mr. Bond.

But the critical storm raised by *Saved* extended itself all over the press: the details of the chief cause of complaint were carefully spelled out. They contributed to the swelling violence which is in our air, and of which we see the results every day of our lives. It is not without significance that the Train Robbers, despite the fact that the guard whom they attacked is still a very sick man, were built into national heroes, symbols of social liberty. If our laws were less absurdly based on property and more upon the value of human life, they would have been given one-third of their sentences and would have lost at least one-third of their haloes.

5 - No Joy to Know Oneself

At this point, again, I want to make my own position clear. I am not speaking for any organized body, for Moral Rearmament, for the "New Puritanism," nor for any such pompous concept as "the people," but entirely for myself as an individual. I have no interest in "clean-up campaigns," which always wreck their own hopes by bringing their sledgehammers to crush ants.

My initial reaction to the realities of the Moors Case, the personalities of the accused, have been slightly modified over the weeks and months intervening: but I have to acknowledge the impact of the initial shock, and there is no point in making oneself seem wiser, more compassionate, than one is.

I think nobody who has read my books could suppose me a prude. In fact, I am not against the description of, or even the stage presentation of, "straight sex," heterosexual or homosexual, if there is feeling in it. Mr. Kenneth Tynan says he would be prepared to see actual copulation on a public stage. Good luck to him, if he can get the audiences to accept it, or hard-working actors—there might

even be a flop one night—to endure it. I am far more concerned with sex-plus-cruelty, sex without feeling.

Sex without emotion is valueless except as a physical
release, and women, few of whom enjoy it much unless
their emotions are involved, come to find this out pretty
soon. This is why so many young women in their teens,
persuaded by young men that if they don't sleep with them
they will become, in Stella Gibbons' phraseology, "with-
ered husks, rinds and gourds," only find bitter disappointment and often develop a hostile attitude towards marriage. This is, in fact, on the part of the young men, a very
old ploy, which was flourishing heartily in the 1940s,
although, judging by present-day illegitimate pregnancy
figures, with not quite so much success.

I do not suggest, either, that physical violence must
not be a part of, or even an integral part of, a play. I admit
that I am tired of the "Gloucester's eyes" argument: this is
a play about filial ingratitude and the blindness of the par-
ent, with *eyes* as a dominant symbol, but it is not primarily
concerned with the blinding of one man, repellent as the
particular episode may be. Indeed, I saw some years ago, at
the Theatre Royal, Stratford, a play called *Whistle in the
Dark*, which was then described by Mr. Tynan, I think, as
"the most uninhibited display of violence upon the London stage." So I went to it—out of professional obligation
—with a sinking heart. *Whistle in the Dark* by Thomas
Murphy was, as it turned out, a genuine deterrent to brutality, not a covert encouragement. This was inherent in
the atmosphere of the play and the skill that went to its
making; a deliberate selective quality was apparent
throughout. It was not a play for "kicks," nor was it designed to be so. It took up a positive moral attitude, which
is something we should all be prepared to do, even at the

risk of error. It is the total abrogation of moral judgment, the "here it is, take it or leave it," the absence (even despite what the writer believes his intention to be) of moral discrimination, which may make a work of literary art into a work of degradation.

I do not mean by this that writers, propounding a problem, are obliged to offer a solution; in fact, I am sure this is not their job. But it should be implicit that they are trying to work towards a solution, that they have themselves a place on which to stand. Tolstoi offers no easy solutions in *War and Peace,* but his own moral feeling pervades the entire novel.

The permissive intellectual's "anything goes" arises partly out of personal vanity. *He* cannot be changed by anything he sees, reads or hears: therefore nobody can be. He is cocooned in a kind of snobbery. He does not really wish to think that depravity exists, since he himself does not feel depraved. He gives exactly the same answer as Brady gave in the dock.* To the permissive, the psychologist can cope with anybody: but few psychologists would agree with him. They have their failures, like the rest of us. They do not pose as medicine-men.

Now we have been brought to a point where, studying Ian Brady and Myra Hindley, we may be compelled to feel that what they have done is less psychotic than "bad": bad in the sense that they did this for the sheer pleasure of doing wrong. After all, most of us do something we know is wrong every day of the week—allow ourselves the joy of malice, drink more than we know we should, neglect the person who needs us because we have something more amusing on foot. Perhaps piffling sins: but they do not make us psychotic. We use psychological excuses because

* See p. 40.

we need to deny the conception of free will, because it is much nicer for us to think we are driven by concealed forces, and so become absolved from personal responsibility for what we do.

On the question of the Sade cult, which reared up at the end of the nineteenth century, fell into abeyance, and has now reappeared, I am in no doubt that it is, and always has been, highly dangerous. Sade was a curious man, more than half mad, and because he was so he suffered all the miseries the eighteenth century thought fit for the insane. Despite the obscene matter in his writings, his only recorded sexual offenses were of a relatively modest and even monotonous kind—for example, inducing prostitutes to whip him and his valet; for practical exercises in self-indulgence, he was not in the same class as Gilles de Retz. His literary talent was slender, his writing utterly turgid except in the pornographic passages, which excited him sufficiently to enable him to put some sort of edge on his prose.

Juliette, for example, is pure sludge, a mixture of sewage and patchouli of no conceivable literary value. It is a ridiculous stringing together of pornographic fantasies which could have no appeal to a balanced reader, but might be finally corrupting to anyone capable of being pushed over the borderline between fantasy and fact. As a stylist, Sade is negligible: compare his style with that of Choderlos de Laclos, who was almost his exact contemporary. As a philosopher, he has a faint appeal for people who are unacquainted with serious philosophic thinking.

(Even Mr. Maurice Girodias does not support Sade wholly on his talents. "De Sade is not a writer of such importance that a ban on his books may be considered as a major loss." Dispraise from this Sir Hubert is dispraise indeed.)

I doubt whether, as a pornographer, Sade is any more harmful than he is as philosopher. For he makes iniquitous ideas sound weighty, almost moral: he manages to get a kind of bogus boom into them.

Consider this famous passage, which was read out at the Moors Trial:

> " 'Is murder a crime in the eyes of Nature?' Doubtless we will humiliate man's pride in reducing him to the ranks of other productions of nature, but nevertheless he is merely an animal like any other, and in the eyes of Nature his death is no more important than that of a fly or an ox. . . . Destruction is Nature's method of progress, and she prompts the murderer to destruction, so that his action shall be the same as plague or famine. . . . In a word, murder is a horror, but a horror often necessary, never criminal, and essential to tolerate in a republic.

It is known that Brady was much given to brooding upon this passage. Is it inconceivable that it may have given him just the rationale, the self-justification, he needed for the acts he had in mind? Surely it is not *quite inconceivable*. And if this even begins to seem possible, then, as I have said before, we need to freshen our thinking upon the subject of mass-availability. We may come to the conclusion that we must take any risk whatsoever in order to preserve the liberty of the writer and his right to be read or for his works to be publicly performed: but at least we have come to the point when we should not, without much thought, merely assume that this is so.

Mr. Girodias writes: "I am not arguing that the works of the infernal Marquis cannot have had any influence *whatsoever* on the tortured mind of the murderer. I am simply trying to show that it was only one of many influences, and presumably one of the weakest by virtue of its speculative and theoretical nature." (But it was, so the facts most strongly suggest, by no means one of the weakest.) Does it make the whole thing better that Brady should have read other such works as well? I cannot see the force of Mr. Girodias' argument. Far less can I comprehend the state of mind which put that word "whatsoever" in italics.

The passage from Sade is, in fact, a prime example of total loss of affect combined with a curious toploftiness, an air of being above the battle. One feels that Sade never saw himself in the rôle of murderee. One also feels that he has never properly thought of the implications of what he is saying. This is really the stuff of fantasy, and silly stuff at that: but it is nevertheless dangerous fantasy, of the kind the Nazis were finally able to put into practice on a mass scale, in the "Final Solution."

It is a mistake for man to feel stronger in his essence than he is. I wanted to attend the Moors Trial: also, I did not. The details of it had already sickened me. My imagination ran too freely. But there is no disguising the fact that a part of me was titillated: I wanted to know *all* the details, not solely because it was my job to do so, but because there was in them an element of repulsive stimulation. I was forced to recognize this, in order to assess the degree of less inhibited stimulation they must have given to many people unconcerned with the affair in any professional sense.

It is probably only people who can recognize consciously the potentiality for cruelty in themselves who truly loathe and detest it in others, since the behavior of others reflects, all too painfully, what they themselves might have been if their natures, also, had been twisted further out of the true.

It is no joy to know oneself, though each of us must try to know. The learning, however, need not consist in deliberate self-exposure to a lavish course of spectacles of cruelty and violence, through every form of mass media. Man is an animal easily conditioned to almost anything, and what we have to fear is that through this sort of exposure our sensibilities may not be made more subtle, but may become blunted.

> Vice is a monster of so frightful mien,
> As, to be hated, needs but to be seen;
> Yet seen too oft, familiar with his face,
> We first endure, then pity, then embrace.*

I knew a young Englishman in the mid-'30s, a research student, whose work took him often to Germany. He happened to be in Nuremberg at the time when the Nazis were publicly degrading Jewish men and women in the streets. This was what he told me.

> The first time it was such a shock, I felt so sick, that I simply took to my heels down the next side-turning.
>
> The second occasion I felt it was my duty to see just what was going on, so I stopped just for a minute. I felt as sick as ever, and did so the third time I tried to watch.
>
> On the fourth I stood in that jeering crowd for quite a while. It seemed awful, but not quite so awful as before, almost as if it was a play. I told myself this was only because I was getting more objective, was able to make a *true* observation of what was being done, so I could warn people when I got home.

* Pope, *Essay on Man.*

Suddenly I realized that I was in serious danger of becoming acclimatized, to feel all this was a part of life, the way things happened. And then I took to my heels for the second time, and I went back to England as soon as I could get my bags packed.

He was a very honest, introspective young man, who had recognized in himself the first tendency to the affectlessness which was poisoning a whole nation, and because he was capable of self-analysis, even into those parts of the mind most of us dread to examine, well—for the second time he took to his heels. For many of us, there might be no second chance to run. I wish I had not forgotten his name, because I shall never forget what he said.

We must never think that *we* are safe, and that therefore everyone else is. None of us is safe. Violence excites me when I see it, as it excites most people: the Theater of Sensation may drive out the Theater of Ideas, but there is a strong demand for the former at the box-office. (Though it is not without interest that a surfeit of this kind of thing has brought audiences flocking back to Shaw, for the relief of enjoying again the Theater of Intelligence.)

How many of us recognize just a tinge of pleasure when we have to punish some yelling termagant of a child? Please—I am not talking about beating it, or even spanking it. Just to deprive it of a promised treat, or to lock it in a room by itself where it can shout and kick as much as it likes, may stir the worm in our loins. Not a few of us have fantasies of violence, fantasies of great revenges; it is our social duty not to bring these even to the borders of action. Does this, then—the restraint—dangerously inhibit us? I shudder to think what has been done, is done daily, by men and women in whom inhibition has broken down.

Some "inhibitions," such as those against theft and murder, are positively good. I do not know why the mere word
should have acquired a bad and wholly unscientific connotation.

My instinct was not wrong in fancying Myra Hindley
as a concentration camp guard. As it turned out, that had
been her own fancy too. Her heroine was Irma Grese,
hanged for war crimes after the overrunning of Belsen,
whose photograph Hindley kept in her room. Brady called
her, as a grisly joke, and with no reference to the late
pianist, his "Myra Hess." I was wrong, however, in imagining her, as I did at first, the dominant partner of these two,
though several other writers and journalists to whom I
talked were taken in by this almost Dostoevskian misdirec-
tion. He read, he led, she followed, until her last moral
scruples were completely trampled down. We must suppose that if she had never met him, her life might have
taken quite a different course, that there was an element of
bad luck in it all. Yet we cannot and must not forget what
it was that she eventually *did*, for that is inescapable. I say
that I could feel no compassion for her at the trial: now I
can feel some pity for what her life is to be. I shouldn't be
surprised, though it seems an improbability now, if she
eventually returns to the Roman Catholic Church.

6 - The Censor and the Self-Censor

Should not the whole question of censorship, and its meaning, be handled with kid gloves?

Maybe. I shan't do so.

There is no censor of books in this country. Matter felt to be undesirable may be submitted, either by police or public, to the Director of Public Prosecutions, who may take legal action or not as he sees fit.

The Lord Chamberlain's office censors plays. This does not seem to be a satisfactory state of affairs, since there is not (there should be) any court of appeal. Nevertheless, the Lord Chamberlain has been surprisingly permissive, though there are lines that he draws. (How can we draw any line? I don't know. But this doesn't mean that we shouldn't make some effort to try. We are all by-passing these issues, through sheer intellectual laziness, or vanity.) On the other hand, he can have his fits of touchiness. His job is a hard one, and basically untenable. I should not feel strongly about the abolition of stage censorship if I really

70

thought that intellectual opinion would let the Public
Prosecutor do his work. If he were not allowed to do so,
our theater would soon come to look like Soho in hard
covers.

Films must be submitted to a board of censors: here,
since the film is a majority art and the theater is not, I suggest that there must rightly be some form of control.
Everyone who seriously disputes this might let his imagination range a little, even if it is only so far as the Night-
town scene of *Ulysses* filmed in its *entirety*, according to its
already perfect film-script.

The form the present film censorship takes is highly
anomalous. In some respects, it has become increasingly
permissive, often to the benefit of the art-form. In other
respects—for instance, the freedom given to the most vulgar and titillative "horror films," which are likely to increase affectlessness in younger people—it might weigh in
with an even heavier hand. I have heard it said that such
films are harmless because audiences "only giggle at
them." That's the whole point: that they do giggle. It
would be better if they sometimes felt sick, and were. The
horror-film cult is detestable because its majority appeal is
to the young or the simple-minded. We often fail to find
these films at all exciting, since we are old enough to find
them silly: and here we must beware of the vanity of middle age, and its failure to form an empathetic relationship
with adolescence.

Television and broadcasting are self-censored. We
might here remind ourselves that "censorship" never
seems such a dirty word when it is we personally who are
the censors. There are still things which, for their good, we
deny and shall continue to deny our children, unless the
climate we live in has driven us mad. I can't think of many

intellectuals who, while preaching total permissiveness, would give Johnny, aged ten, half a dozen Dexedrine tablets if he demanded them, or procure for Sarah, aged twelve, her first reefer. All adults exercise some censorship, upon themselves and those dependent upon them, every day of their lives.

The amount of violence and cruelty on the television screen seems to me not so great as is generally thought, though there is still far too much of it. True, certain oddities slip through, such as a play in which a young lout intrudes upon a perfectly harmless, if stuffy, middle-class group in their home and proceeds to smash that home up with an axe, presumably to the entire satisfaction of the author. I do not regard the "Western" film as cruel, nor even perniciously violent, in the sense I mean it: it always takes a strong moral attitude—so strong it might be written out in capital letters of chalk upon a blackboard—and is as formal as a Japanese Noh play. So let us not waste too much time here.

I do not wish to see the slightest extension of the present forms of censorship or near-censorship, nor, until the effects of total license have had a serious public examination, do I want to see them relaxed. The picture we present, in some areas of the arts, is quite grimy enough as it is.

But we must not forget that two censorships are always in operation: with plays, that of the producing company; with books, that of the publisher. It is the business of both to exercise self-restraint and to refuse to be badgered into producing material which they themselves find offensive, simply out of a mob frenzy to be "with it," whatever that "it" may at the moment be.

I am disposed to believe that this is the only thing

which might make for a positive amelioration of our present problems, offering, if not a solution—and I have not set myself to propound solutions—a small contribution towards one. It is of no use for us to expect a change of heart, or even fresh consideration of the whole matter, from those at the receiving end. The mere phrase "the public" is an abstraction: "the public" is not a kind of corporate mind to which one can address appeals, certainly not on matters of aesthetics and morals. If we believe new thinking is necessary, we must address ourselves to those who are the purveyors, whose primary responsibility it is to disseminate what they believe to be valuable, and therefore good. Nobody else has any control whatsoever.

Many London publishers are disturbed by the curious performances of Mr. Maurice Girodias, who permits himself, if I am not wrong, to be described as a publisher of pornography. He is scarcely, to put it mildly, reflecting luster on their profession. But there is no doubt that *any* publicly expressed attitude towards absolute license is found by some people—usually very vocal people—to be intoxicating. They have a wonderful sense of freedom, a sense almost physical: they would like to shout and wave their arms about. So it is hard for the publisher, under pressure from such as these, to keep his head and say No. He has every right to say No: he cannot be forced to publish a book he doesn't want, even though it is a great smutty 400,000-word success by some heroin-taking Johnny-come-lately (Americans seem to feel it is better to arrive late than just to arrive) in the United States. Yet I do not doubt that there are extreme libertarians who would like to see him *forced* to do this. There is a tyranny of libertarianism as well as of restriction, and we can already hear its baying, and the rolling of its tumbrils.

The producer and the publisher have a very heavy responsibility towards the health of the society in which they live. There are some who feel the weight an increasingly great one to bear, but who will continue honorably to bear it.

Robert Lusty, managing director of Hutchinson, replied to Mr. Girodias as follows:

> May I be allowed to differ? The Moors Trial did not "add a new and rather sinister aspect to the old debate on 'freedom of expression.'" There is in fact nothing new about it. What it most certainly did do was to explode the disclaimers and persuasions of those who write and publish without regard to the social consequences. It also, and with terrifying emphasis, underlined once again the responsibilities which confront those who have editorial decisions to make, when either writing or publishing.

By the by, I believe in absolute freedom for the press under the sanction of the law. If I had not believed this before, I should have believed it since the reporting of the Moors Trial, which was, with only a few exceptions, impeccable in its restraint and decency.

7 - Trying to Understand

"No-ah," "no-ah," "no-ah." That was how Myra Hindley denied everything. She made a stolid showing in the witness-box. Let us not deny her the virtue of courage: we do not know what these long, long weeks in the remand prison were like, and we cannot guess. The girl who dyed and set her hair: did she speak to Myra? Did Myra speak to her? What had they to say to each other?

The jury was surprisingly young. Five of the jurymen looked no more than thirty years of age and may have been less. One, a middle-aged man, turned half-sideways and stared at Hindley from time to time with a half-smile, as if unable to believe that she was a real person. The judge was quiet, quiet, and invariably courteous to the accused. So was the attorney-general, prosecuting.

The public at the back of the court were so still that there seemed no need for two policemen to sit *facing* them: a man cried out once—the only disturbance of any kind in the whole course of the trial—and that was to encourage a frightened little girl, a relation, to speak up and not be afraid. In the Gallery for Distinguished Visitors, the women in flowery hats struck a slightly incongruous note: yet nobody there seemed to have been attending the trial either for frivolous or for lubricious reasons. All was matter-of-fact gravity.

The exhibits were on a large table, packed in plastic bags, cardboard soap-boxes. They looked very domestic. This might have been a stall at a jumble sale, with the vicar's wife presiding. The tape-recorders were there, the clothes of the buried, Smith's stick, still stained with blood, the axe—that axe which, the accuser said, happened to be kept in the fireplace of the living room.

Why?

To mend a broken table with.

There was, in the court, no atmosphere of horrific excitement, except when those terrible tapes were played. The horror was a stony one. Only the nurturing of an inward chill could anesthetize some of the loathsomeness which made pressmen, at the end of each day, almost euphoric with the sheer relief of getting out into the streets.

In the witness-box, Hindley was impassive. Most of the time, her chin was propped up by one long white hand, while the other was splayed out across the ledge. She hated us all, judge, jury, pressmen: she did not yet seem to hate herself. But was this hate or fear? The most unfeeling have feeling for themselves, and to sit in isolation like this, for five and a half hours, aware of the flow of repulsion from everyone in the court, must have been an experience hard for us to imagine. Possibly she had little time to think of fear, but thought only of battling as best she might with the cross-examination.

Her voice at first was breathy and toneless, the flat North of England "no-ah, "no-ah," splitting the monosyllable, dripped on like rain from the eaves or a tap that needs fixing. Later it gained depth; the breathiness turned almost to the professional huskiness of the actress. Like Brady, she was a good stone-waller. No, she wasn't there. She didn't know anything about it. She had nothing to do with it.

She was not a good liar. Why did she threaten to hit the child? Because she wanted to stop her screaming; the doors and windows were open.

Oddly enough, there was no cross-examination on this point. Doors and windows open, on a freezing Boxing Night? Why?

Her slippers were shown to her, checked flatties, brown and white, now blotched with Evans' blood. Oh, but those are not the ones she was wearing that evening. They simply happened to be in the sitting room. What was she wearing, then? The ones she now has on. She took off a spotless white shoe with a medium stiletto heel and offered it for inspection. What, did she walk on the moors in those? She replied, she always took the car. The attorney-general asked her to remark the fact that there was no blood inside the shoes, which there might well have been had they been lying, empty, in the living room. With frowning care, as if she herself were a forensic witness, a Spilsbury, a Simpson, Hindley took quite a time to examine the linings. But no, she persisted, these were not the ones she was wearing.

It is a peculiar fact that whenever there was a stir in the courtroom at all (even so, it was no more than the sudden, scarcely perceptible ripple of a cornfield on a day that is almost still) this was not in response to some horror, but rather to some more than commonly callous or preposterous lie.

She never even saw what was happening to Lesley Ann Downey during the photographic session, though she was in the room. She was standing looking out of the window, playing the radio. No, she saw nothing at all. The ripple came then.

I saw her display some shadowy emotion on three occasions. First, there was a touch of anger when she told us how, when the police took her to an interview room, she was confronted with a giant poster of John Kilbride. Unfair! You could feel her inwardly screaming it.

The second time was when she looked at her mother, while that poor woman was giving evidence: it was the first time I saw Hindley look directly at anyone but judge and lawyers. We show very little of our feelings on the surface, when the will is in control: the mother, a small, grey, dignified woman, must have been in a nightmare of shame and terror; yet all she showed was simple grief. The daughter began to stare at her—the mesomorphic stare so characteristic of Hindley—as if she were trying to exercise hypnosis. Was she hoping for help, from this quarter at least?

Mrs. Hindley did her best. Of Smith—"Maureen used to be frightened of her husband. . . ." "He can be good when he wants to be, but half the time he's a very bad lad." But there was poor hope for Myra in these touching attempts to turn Smith into Svengali.

The ordeal of Mrs. Hindley was mercifully short. She left the box with the same sorrowing dignity as she had entered, a small figure to suggest Greek tragedy, but suggest it she somehow did.

So little appears on the surface of any of us. We are far more secret than we think, which is why we have a moral responsibility for the nature of those secrets we choose to carry within us.

The third time Hindley looked up, she looked at me. I was directly facing her, and as it happened was the only woman in the press-box. She caught my gaze and she held it, dark doll's eyes in the porcelain face steady and burning. I am not at all given to Gothic romanticism: yet those few moments, when I was willing her to look away, filled me with fright. She soon got tired of me, and her gaze fell.

She was hating me. From her point of view, why not? I was up there, in safety. She was in the witness-box and would soon be returned to the dock. I was going to walk out into the busy shopping streets, to be anonymous under the grey sky among the rain-damped crowds. She was going, though not to die, to a condition of life none of us could imagine. She was thinking, I believe, "Well, it could have been you, couldn't it?"

Here I think we have to consider the *humani nil a me alienum puto* concept without false romanticism, and without posturing. No, it could not have been me. I could do, and do do, many bad things, but my instincts do not lie in the direction of Hindley's. There are not, thank God, a great number of people who, their normal sadistic propensities being overstimulated, will ever pass the borderline of reason and put those instincts to practical purpose. If the number were great, we should see the hell of Hieronymus Bosch opening all around us. But there are some men and women—perhaps more than we think—who may be driven by various pressures into this kind of madness (I shall return later to what degree of "madness" there was in this particular case) and we should see that those pressures which it is in our own power to lessen, are lessened.

As I implied earlier in this book, I do not think we do much good by pretending false empathy. It hinders any attempt to see the facts as they are, and inhibits what hope we may have of reaching that possible degree of psycholog-ical understanding which may come with time. For it is the Bradys and Hindleys we must control somehow; we must also help them, if they can be helped. We shall not do it by pretending that under any pressures, short, perhaps, of those of Nazi Germany, all of us might have done as they did. This, to anyone who witnessed this trial, would seem mere attitudinizing.

In his final article on the case, Francis Wyndham * entered a very subtle *caveat:*

> Both showed remarkable control which, in the cir-cumstances, could only be construed as callousness. But there was nothing heroic about their defiance: it was rooted in lack of imagination, the ultimate mediocrity. In years to come, some myth may form around the mem-ory of this couple who explored the sensation of evil to its furthest limits—a cult like the recent attempt to vindi-cate the "theories" of de Sade. It would be based on a dangerous error. These acts of destruction were neither super-human nor sub-human; for all their hideous ex-travagance they were mean. In spite of its outrageous material coupled with scrupulous formality, this "sensa-tional" trial seemed to have a hollow centre where the accused should have been. It was almost as though they were being tried by proxy, ghostly presences in an empty dock, as dead as their victims on the moors.

Yes: we may be capable of Saint-making again, just as we have sanctified Sade. We should keep careful watch for the first straw in that particular wind.

I have tried, in this book, not to emphasize the abominations of this case more than is absolutely necessary for the understanding of what I am saying: but I hope

* *The Sunday Times*, May 8, 1966.

these abominations will not be forgotten—not a single detail of them *; if they are, then the familiar sanctification campaign should soon get under way.

Let us not forget that not only did they tape-record the sadistic murder of the child, Lesley Ann Downey, but that Hindley induced another little girl to talk to her about the search for her friend's body—and she tape-recorded that. There is a sort of technological squalor here which is not easily associated with Apostles of Freedom brave enough to put their principles into practice. There was nothing brave about any of it. As Francis Wyndham says, all of it was mean. Wretched, dirty and mean.

What about the inevitable question—how far did the environmental defects of our society make Hindley and Brady what they are? If we consider the careers of both, the easy answer becomes a complex one.

Brady's youth had all the classic background for the breeding of a criminal. Illegitimate, never knowing his father, born in the Gorbals, he was brought up by an apparently good foster-mother, who seems to have made no discrimination between him and her own four children. Yet in the end she found herself unable to cope with him. By ten, he was torturing cats and burying them alive. A childhood friend who remembers him comments: "The cats weren't worth bothering with after he'd finished with them. He always carried a flick-knife and was a great one for a carry-on." It was this same friend whom Brady tied to a post, then stacked newspapers around his feet and set fire to them. An amateurish job, and the victim got away.

At this point, let me offer the reminder, to blanket-thinkers, that most illegitimate children born in the

* Though the full reality of these has been grasped—owing to the restraint of court and of press—by very few.

Gorbals and brought up in foster-homes, do *not* become torturers by the age of ten: nor, even, do bad children who torture animals often turn out to be multiple murderers.

Not surprisingly, Brady was unpopular at school. A remote boy, bad at football, but bookish and embryonically musical, he became obsessed by Nazism. When he was old enough he took to house-breaking, making his first court appearance at thirteen, on a charge of house-breaking and attempted theft. He made his second at fourteen. Two more years' probation, the condition being made that he should now return to his real mother. (Magistrates have a touching belief in the absolute value of the blood-tie.) In 1955 he appeared before the Manchester courts for stealing lead seals, and this time he was sent to Borstal. On his release in 1958, he worked at a variety of occupations, as a brewer's laborer, a porter in the Manchester fruit market, and at last as a £12-per-week invoice clerk at Millward's Merchandise. For some years he had been drinking heavily.

Yes, it is a miserable record, and there was much in his upbringing that we have to pity.

But, I repeat, thousands upon thousands with such an upbringing have not done murder, certainly not of such a sort. Here I wish we knew as much of the genetic as of the environmental background, for from this we might derive our maximum source of understanding. We all accept the fact that a poet is born, not made. For some reason, we are leery of applying any such tag to the habitual criminal, though it could provide the main prop of his defense— under the eye of God, if not of the law.

For Myra Hindley, however, life ran quite differently. She was a war-baby (as a good many of our children are), born in Gorton, Manchester, in 1942. Her father was a paratrooper, and a Roman Catholic, her mother a Protestant. After the birth of her sister Maureen, she went to live with her grandmother in a back-to-back only two hundred yards away from her home.

She was, a school friend said of her, "always laughing and singing," making up jokes, playing the mouth-organ: but her school reports described her personality as "not very sociable," and her attendances as "consistently unsatisfactory." There is some conflict of opinion here.

She was bad at needlework and domestic science, good at games. She does not appear to have been unpopular with her fellows.

In 1957, she attended the funeral of a boy of thirteen found drowned in a local reservoir. The effect of this child's death seems to have been profound; why it should have taken such a singular hold on Hindley's imagination we do not know. Hitherto left to herself to make up her mind about religion, she now, in 1958, chose to be confirmed as a Roman Catholic.

She was not a stupid girl. Although she failed the 11-plus, she had an I.Q. of 109, which is slightly above the norm. Before she left school at fifteen, she had written a book of sixty pages, which was put into the school library. Although I should like to see it, I doubt whether it would tell us much. It is the sheer persistence of the effect which is interesting: few girls write sixty pages just for fun. We must sense some strong aspiration here which was never satisfied.

From that time until her first contact with Brady, she lived a normal teenage life—dances, cinemas, chasing the boys. She was a good and patient baby-sitter. As we know, you could always trust your toddlers to her, and go out to Bingo with a quiet mind.

No police record. Nothing unusual in her background, except for the dividing of the two sisters between the two houses, with the two hundred yards' gap.

No environmental judgment can be drawn, then, from her case on the facts as we know them. Was she no more than a victim of corruption by a wicked man? There may be much we do not know, and I suspect that there is a great deal. But it was certainly ill luck for her that she met him at all. He passed on to her the ideas stimulated in him, already a creature of criminal instincts and behavior, by what he read and doubtless by what he saw in the cinema or on the television screen. It is significant that on the first occasion when they went out together, he took her to a film of the Nuremberg rallies.

8 - What's Left?

None of the ideas I have already set out in this book, as to whether evil communications do in fact corrupt good manners, has any political relevance whatsoever. These questions are the concern of all of us, no matter whether we stand on the right, or the left, or in the center. Yet attempts to protest against the concept that total license may produce an irresponsible society have been obfuscated by a misconception, that the cause of "total permissiveness" is somehow left-wing.

I have emphasized that the views I am setting out are personal views. Since I have held serious political convictions all my adult life, many of them well to the left, I want to discuss this misconception at none too great a length.

It is, in fact, a dangerous misconception, if we believe that total permissiveness really does present a problem and a peculiarly intractable problem, to the whole society. Once the notion becomes common, as a kind of stereotype, that total permissiveness is equivalent to left-wing thinking, then we are split down the middle and lose our social energies. Some people will be advocating total permissiveness as a symbol of progress—i.e., they will be reaching wrong conclusions (if the argument in this essay is substantial) for creditable reasons. Others will be criticizing total permissiveness merely *because* they consider it a symbol of progress—i.e., they will be reaching right conclusions for reasons not so creditable.

The truth is a great deal more complicated. At one extreme, the condition is obvious enough. No *revolutionary* left-wing society can even begin to contemplate total permissiveness. This has been demonstrated by historical fact. It is also evident by the most rudimentary social analysis. The Soviet Union is in most respects more puritanical than the West, and has been so for over a generation. It is now becoming somewhat more relaxed, but no one who knows modern Russia can believe that it is going to approximate to our western situation within foreseeable time. This is not a result of individual or bureaucratic caprice: even less is it a result of the Russians being naturally more prudish than we are. On the contrary. So far as these generalizations mean anything, they are a very hearty people. No, the explanation is simpler and more general. A society in the process of radical change, by a kind of natural law, seems to impose upon itself a rigid code of expression and behavior. This has been the case in transformations within capitalist countries; compare the English and American nineteenth century. It has been much more strongly marked in socialist revolutions. The most extreme example of all is contemporary China.

It is clear, then, that citizens in socialist countries (in the full sense) have to accept a degree of constraint that we in the West have forgotten. This is particularly true of anything connected with the written word. Western writers and western readers have for the last ten or fifteen years been experiencing an absence of constraint such as has never happened before in human history (some periods of expression were sexually free, as in early imperial Rome, but not at all politically free; the same was true of Restoration England). Whether this total absence of constraint is good for literature remains to be proved. So far, the greatest literature (that of Periclean Athens, Elizabethan England, nineteenth-century Russia) has been produced in circumstances of moderately strong, but not overwhelming, authoritarian pressure. However, that is another subject and we have to cope with our own time.

I should find it bizarre for any English, American or French writer to feel that he would write more happily in China, or even in the Soviet Union (where literary freedom has genuinely expanded within the last five years despite apparent setbacks), than in his own country. We ourselves have the freedom to write, in any political terms, and to a large extent in any sexual terms, without being in danger of jail, or even of social disapproval. Therefore, is there no obligation on us to pay for these privileges, by the exercise of some sort of moral responsibility? Do we want everything for nothing?

It used to be customary in certain circles, and indeed is today customary among a vestigial few, to say grace before and after meat. We have the freedom to write almost precisely what we choose, with certain reservations regarding that mystery of "hard-core" pornography, and regarding plain sedition: blasphemy, I fancy, is out of the running. We encounter no risks to our bodies by so doing, and little risk to our respective psyches through the thunder of public opinion, which in our case will lie doggo. But having this license, ought we not to "say grace"—i.e., express our gratitude—by realizing the leaden weight of the liberties now upon our shoulders? We have been given almost ultimate personal responsibility, in aesthetic terms, for what we say and do. Is it right that we should shrug off that responsibility, gobble up the plentiful meal which our system of society has offered us, without the slightest indication that, in return, something is owing from us? It should be expressed, this gratitude, by the careful thought of each of us concerning what he writes, why he writes a thing, how he writes a thing. We have grown sufficiently intelligent to put an arm down into the deep-freeze of our unconscious minds and drag out motive, however concealed it may be by the frost around it. The autocrats have gone. Is it unreasonable to think that we should exercise some autocracy, each and every one of us, upon ourselves?

It may help us in this exercise if we analyze the forces which, in our contemporary western society, have removed —from all forms of verbal expression—almost any kind of constraint. This removal of constraint at present only occurs in advanced industrial societies, and (as we can see from the example of the Soviet Union, which is now an advanced industrial society) even these require a particular kind of politico-economic structure. In fact, removal of constraint appears to need either a free-enterprise economy like that of the U.S.A. or a mixed economy like our country's or Sweden's. These countries demonstrate the characteristic examples of verbal emancipation. The societies have many political features, and one essential economic feature, in common, and it is almost certain that the same loosening forces have been at work.

The first of these arises, paradoxically, from the comparatively static nature of the society itself. In very slightly different forms—the resemblances are more important than

the differences here—the American society, the British society, the Swedish society, appear to have reached a kind of
plateau. Further change, for a considerable period, will be
minimal compared with the changes that have gone before. I mean, *real* changes, in terms of serious politics—and
in those terms, these societies are abnormally far removed
from any kind of revolutionary disturbance. What is more,
a very large proportion of the population is, within the
human limits, content with the plateau that has been
reached.

Now, many people don't like admitting that they are
content. It is often good that they don't. Often I wish that
on major things they were less so. But on the comfortable
Anglo-American, Scandinavian plateau, they have tended
to drift away from major things, and not to find a major
cause. Not having found a major cause, they proceed to in-
vest great emotional energy in minor ones: and of the
minor ones, verbal emancipation has taken a high place.
The constraints that an emerging society (such as that of
the nineteenth century) had, by the nature of its social
tasks, imposed upon itself—they were constraints which a
static society could protest against. It was an easy subject
for protest, it channeled sexual energy, it made people feel
free, just by the theme of the operation. It is remarkable, if
we look back two generations, to see how much intense
passion has been expended in this one cause. With the
same amount of passion spent on social purposes, America
might now have a Health Service, and Britain might be
able to earn a living. But this was a protest not designed
for social change. To some, it was designed, maybe without
their knowing it, to evade any social change at all.

In others, the emotion which supported verbal emancipation was entirely generous, benevolent with the sweet-

ness of liberal optimism. That is a real sweetness, though we have learned too much these forty years to trust liberal optimism, or build our hopes upon it. It still leaves its traces, though, on many of us. If people are left alone, free to express themselves, then they will be happier and better: that has been believed by good people; it lies beneath what Philip Rieff calls "the triumph of the therapeutic." And, on the plateau of comfortable society, where for the first time the brute necessities of living have been largely met, the belief has been acted upon by people of good will of all kinds of formal political opinion.

Those two forces, the need for progress, the diffuse, optimistic *laissez faire,* have worked together. With them, there is another, nothing like so respectable-sounding, which also, though prevented in more regulated societies, can operate in ours. That is, the simple desire to make money. In a free-enterprise economy, or a mixed economy, persons can't be stopped from making money unless they are doing social harm. Usually, most of us accept that they shouldn't be. Occasionally we carry this process so far as to prove that, though some misguided critics might consider they were doing social harm, actually this is quite untrue. The classical example of this attitude is the defense of the free sale of firearms in various American states. To some touchy people, such as myself, this trade might appear to be dangerous to a lunatic extent, and irresponsibly mercenary: but that, we are told, shows the narrowness of our vision. . . .

Well, let us be blunt. Sex is an easy sell. Sadistic sex is the easiest of all sells. A good many people can expect, out of unlimited verbal emancipation, to make a quick killing (the idiom has a sardonic ring). This is unavoidable in our kind of society. But it would be helpful if people engaged in these discussions behaved as they would have to behave in the House of Commons, and "disclose their interests." One of the oddities of the entire situation is that, in becoming so unprudish about sex, we have suddenly become extravagantly prudish about money. We ought also to remember that these particular considerations could not apply in a non-commercial society.

I am not for an instant suggesting that the great majority of those who believe in ultimate verbal emancipation have a monetary interest, either direct or indirect. On the contrary, I am sure that their motives are honest. But I am suggesting that the politics of the whole controversy are unusually complex. They cut right across divisions between left and right in ordinary political terms, they are as divorced from serious politics of the right as much as of the left. In the long run, they depend upon the model of the society one is trying to build: and upon the human and social assumption on which one is trying to build it.

9 - *What Do We Do Next?*

At the end of the case Mr. Elwyn Jones (no relation to his namesake, the attorney-general) wrote this *:

> If a trial is a drama, then that at Chester has lacked climax and catharsis. The trial stopped rather than ended. The judge said, rapidly, "Put him down." He spoke two more sentences, then said, "Put her down."
> . . .
> The trial was over and we who had followed it were drained empty of response. It would be absurd to deny that, in this case, three concurrent sentences of life imprisonment for Brady and two plus seven years accorded to Hindley were emotionally ineffectual. I am not certain that they are intellectually satisfactory, either, if their result is to set [for] the prison system a major security problem.

I shall never forget the exhilaration of being in the crowded gallery of a crowded House of Lords when capital punishment was finally abolished by a majority of one hundred votes. Peers, young and old, had jostled into the

* *The Sunday Telegraph,* May 8, 1966.

lobbies, flowing in their opposing streams like counter-
marchers at a gym-display. Some, such as the Earl of Hare-
wood, had formally taken their seats only a day or so
before, in order to register their votes against the death
penalty. The feeling, to me, was of a sudden cleansing and
freshening: as if the windows had been thrown open upon
a stuffy room, and the air of the sea had poured in.

Yet Elwyn Jones is right. When the Moors Trial
ended we did feel a lack of catharsis: something violent
should have happened to put an end to violence. Throughout, *we were missing the shadow of the rope*. The end was,
in fact, unaesthetic.

Do not think I am saying that we should kill in order
to produce a work of art. I am as strong against capital
punishment as I have ever been, as glad to be rid of it as I
was that night in the House of Lords. Why—if this were
the only reason—should I ask someone to do something
filthy that I would not do myself? Joseph de Maistre,
Sardinian envoy to St. Petersburg in 1802 and supreme
philosophical reactionary, made a real point when he compared the public approval of the office of executioner with
the social dread and hatred extended to the man himself,
though he did not draw from this the same conclusion that
I draw.

Several times during the hearing, I found myself
thinking, as the Medusa face of Hindley, under the melon
puffball of hair, stared hour after hour from the witness-
box, that if those two could have been caught red-handed
(remembering Evans, the cliché here makes one shudder)
and simply shot down, it would have been better for everybody, better for those who will have the dreadful anxiety
of punishing *and protecting* them, and infinitely better for
the public, which, despite the real and deliberate discre-

tion of the press, had been plunged for three weeks in a bath of sewage. I felt just the same about the war criminals in the Nuremberg trials.

Is this advocacy of lynch-law? But I am not advocating at all the validity of the emotions I say that I felt. They are wrong ones. I am trying to make clear the extraordinary psychological effect this case must have had on any introspective spectator. It threw us all out of kilter: some of the badness rubbed off on us, all of us felt unclean.

I do not mean for a moment that we should feel, each and every one of us, in some way personally "responsible" for the deaths of the young man and the two children; there was no reason for us "all" to feel personally responsible for the death of poor Marilyn Monroe. I distrust these collective pronouns.

We were far too alienated in feeling towards the whole trial for that. Even in the fairly small courtroom, I kept having the impression that Hindley and Brady were *a long way off,* divided from me by something like a thin fog. Their faces seemed to advance or to recede, to bloat or to diminish, as one's own emotions fluctuated.

Away from the house at Hattersley, jerked out of the strange dimension that had been theirs into one that was ours, they hardly seemed real at all. They looked real enough, or Brady did: but because we knew what they had done, somehow they were not. They did not seem, in that court, even part of the trial: they were like visitors from another planet, disconnected from our lives. That is why sympathy became virtually impossible, empathy totally so.

But there is no question that the reform of the law has left us, as Mr. Jones says, with a major security problem.

One thing the "ordinary" criminal will not tolerate (the habitual shoplifter, the petty larcenist, the house-

breaker) is the prisoner convicted of sexual offenses towards children, or of child-murder. Sooner or later they
will take their own revenge, and it is almost impossible to
stop them. The problem is not that this couple, unlike the
Train Robbers, are likely to have friends eager to organize
their escape: it is that while they are in jail we are, and
must be, concerned for their own safety. While Hindley is
in Holloway, watch will have to be kept to see that she is
not beaten up by her fellow-prisoners. But you can't watch
forever, any more than you can watch the cat and the
canary, and those fellow-prisoners will wait.

As for Brady, this will apply also, though there are
prisons that may be better adapted for his protection than
Holloway for Myra Hindley's.

So what do we do? We cannot keep them indefinitely
in solitary confinement or they will go mad, and it is no
part of the law's punishment to drive a man and woman
insane.*

The history of penal reform is largely a record of good
men propounding bad solutions for the right reasons.
From Bentham's panopticon prison, a high-minded device
for achieving supervision of prisoners at all times, to the
solitary-confinement jail built by the architect John Havi-
land in the area of Philadelphia in the 1830s and backed
by the Quakers on the grounds that the prisoner would be
kept from corrupt fellows, given the chance to protect his
good resolutions and time to brood over his errors and
make peace with God, nothing has really worked.

The concept of the penal settlement, with its attendant
horrors, has now become untenable: yet within that system
there arose one good and compassionate man, who made

* At the time of writing (July 21, 1966), Brady, who is in Durham
Prison, has elected to remain alone.

out of a hell a place of genuine reform and self-respect.*

Captain Alexander Maconochie was born in 1787, of a good Scots family. He was destined for the law, but decided to join the navy. In 1810 he was captured by the French when the ship in which he served as a lieutenant was wrecked by a storm, and he remained a prisoner-of-war till Napoleon abdicated. It may have been this experience which turned him to the study of penal reform in Van Diemen's Land more than a quarter of a century later.

He was, with others, instrumental in forming the Royal Geographical Society: in 1833 he became first Professor of Geography in University College, London, and held the position till he left for Van Diemen's Land in 1837.

The conditions of Norfolk Island, off the coast of Tasmania, were appalling. The island was designed for men who had been transported from England to Australia, had been convicted and sentenced a second time: regarded as totally irreclaimable, they were sent to the ultimate place of terror. Maconochie was appointed to Norfolk Island as governor in 1839. Before taking up the post, he had written a memorandum which remains a model of humanity and good sense to this day.

He worked by a *mark system,* which inflicted not a time-sentence but a labor-sentence. The convicts could earn back their freedom by hard work. "It teaches self-denial, by enabling them to purchase a speedier termination to their slavery by the social qualities, and makes the prisoners themselves coadjutors in the preservation of discipline, by giving them an interest in each other's good

* The facts of this story are taken from the study of Maconochie by the Hon. Mr. Justice John Vincent Barry, chairman of the Department of Criminology in the University of Melbourne.

behavior; and lastly, it prepares them for restoration to society, by gradually relaxing the restraints on their conduct and training their powers of self-governance."

Captain Maconochie's convicts were treated as laborers, with marks for wages: a certain number of these had to be earned as a condition of discharge. They also had an alternative value: a man could either buy a deduction of so many days from his sentence, or he could buy food. During the first stage, the prisoners worked under stringent discipline. During the second, they might form themselves into companies of six, and work for a common fund of marks. (Maconochie hoped, by this means, to implant social feelings into the selfish.) In the last stage, the parties were dispersed: each man now had his own hut and garden and, if he wished, might keep pigs or poultry.

The gallows were destroyed. The lash fell into almost total disuse. Maconochie, as an act of faith, removed the protective bars from his own house. The men no longer wore convict clothes, and the governor walked openly with his family among them. On the Queen's Birthday, in 1840, he gave them a day's holiday, with sports, theatrical performances and a small tot of rum and lemonade in which they might drink the monarch's health.

When the news of this modest gala reached London, there was a great rumpus. The retributive penologists had been out for his blood for a long time past, and the uproar, combined with an incident in 1842 when some convicts tried to seize a brig, led to his recall in 1844. He was replaced by a Major Childs, who promptly dismantled the reform system, restored lash, leg-irons and gallows, and in a short time Norfolk Island took on its old, familiar aspect of a hell-hole, as dreadful as it had been before Maconochie came. One feels the most profound pity for those convicts who lived through the transition period. The island was abandoned as a penal settlement in 1856.

The slander was, of course, that under Maconochie the place had been full of mutiny and murder. This was totally untrue. During his period as governor, about 1,450 prisoners were discharged and the percentage of re-convictions had fallen to less than three per cent. Out of 920 old lags, who had been judged beyond hope, only twenty were known to be re-convicted. "It was a proud boast, as well as evidence of sound reformation, for a former convict to be able to say he was 'one of Captain Maconochie's men.' "

I recommend this story to those interested in prison reform. It may be found, with other essays, in *Pioneers in Criminology,* edited by Hermann Mannheim (Stevens and Sons, London, 1960).

A great part of Maconochie's success was due, of course, to the fact that he was working in a colony—i.e., in open space—and not within a closed prison. Space is an obvious prerequisite for piggeries for all. Yet the marks system would seem an excellent incentive to reform, and so, on Norfolk Island, it proved. I am quite sure that our greatest hope for regenerating the criminal is to provide him with work of an intrinsically valuable and socially productive nature.

But what are the trade unions going to say? I hope they will provide a generous answer, in order to help those who may not have their liberty again for years to come, perhaps, in some cases, never: and will do so not with the idea that this must eventually weaken organized industry, but with the desire to give a new hope and dignity to our whole society.

10 - "Life"

At some time or other in the lives of most of us, we find ourselves accidentally locked in a room. A bolt has jammed, a handle has loosened, a key refuses to turn. Our *immediate* instinct is to panic. We shall be locked in forever. We are prisoners, and for life.

Intellectually, we know that this is most unlikely. A friend will hear us and come to the rescue, perhaps a porter, if we live in a block of flats: perhaps a passer-by. At worst it will be the fire-brigade, and though we shall lose face as we clamber backwards out of that window, we shall be free again. The second instinct is to be very calm, to sit down and turn our minds to the problem ahead of us. In a moment, we will try again to open that door, taking the job quietly and steadily. We may even delay action for a few minutes while we smoke a cigarette, look at a newspaper, study the pattern of a curtain. Panic has gone. Then we begin coolly to attend to the business of our release, and we fail. We try again and again, each time more frantically, and again we fail. So we begin to shout.

At first we try to attain a clear, jocular tone, indicat-

ing nothing but a sort of rueful amusement at this particular example of the human predicament, or at the malice of
inanimate objects. Nobody comes. We shout louder, and
this time the note is not so rich in jocularity. We end up
by shouting in a way which is quite unmistakable, the
shouting of panic. It is probably the strength lent by panic
to the noise we are making which finally attracts attention
and rescue.

The door opens, we are let out. For half an hour we
may feel a little shaken: then we forget about it. For we
knew all the time, didn't we, that we were not in the
slightest danger of life-imprisonment?

Imagine what it is like to be locked in, not by acci-
dent, but by punitive design, not knowing when you are to
be released or, in terms of the law as it now stands,
whether you ever will be. I am not sure myself that I can
imagine more than the panic.

There seems to be no crime for which the penalty of
life-imprisonment should not be enough, bearing with it
the total destruction of family ties, the wreckage of normal
sexual behavior, the tearing away of all social dignity.
That is, it should seem enough, if we do not primarily seek
retribution: and for the murders of Lesley Ann Downey
and John Kilbride, I think there can be no retribution.

"The rope's too good for them, after what they did."
Yet no penalty would, in terms of retribution, the revenge
of society, have seemed adequate: which is precisely why
any application of the *lex talionis,* even had it been a practical possibility, would in this case have no meaning.

Still, there was in that courtroom the normal human
impulse to see *something* happen to them. People felt at
the time that the attorney-general, who conducted the
prosecution with the maximum of skill and restraint, was

too "soft" with Hindley. They wanted to see someone break her down. I wanted to see it myself. This was partly a vengeful feeling, and partly the feeling of sheer frustration at being unable to understand what was going on behind that pink and white mask.

The very long, or even endless, sentence of imprisonment must be thought of primarily in terms of the protection of society. From such people as Brady and Hindley, society needs to be protected very much indeed.

"Would you think in such moderate terms if Lesley had been your child?" No, of course not, and I should have been *inhuman* if I'd done so. But I should not then have been sound in judgment. For those who have known cruelty of the most depraved nature wreaked upon people they love, whether these are children or adults, the only catharsis is the fantasy of an eye for an eye. But this is, and must remain, a fantasy.

The rest of us, not personally involved, have to think how we can so order our society that these horrors shall not happen again, and the first thing we have to do is to put our dangerous criminals under restraint.

Which leads us back to the "life" sentence.

What does it now mean, and what will it mean in this case?

As Giles Playfair points out, the average person thinks it means being let out again after nine years. When the bodies of Lesley Ann and John Kilbride were found, even after Hindley and Brady had been arrested, mothers over an enormous area, even so far as Coventry and Nuneaton, kept their children indoors, never letting them stray beyond the garden gate, or even to play unwatched in the garden. They were terrified that more murderers of this kind still remained free; now they are terrified that these two, in a few years, will again be loosed upon society. The law as it stands means that Brady and Hindley may not be released without the consent of the Home Secretary, after consultation with the Lord Chief Justice, who may in turn consult the trial judge.

This seems to me vague enough, in abstract, to be in this particular case a cause for terror, though I am certain it will not prove so in practice. A life-sentence can, and does, sometimes mean precisely what it says. But in any event, the present uncertainty of the law in such an instance of multiple and corporate murder cannot help but cause bewilderment and unease.

It has to be remembered, of course, that the main purpose of the prison sentence is, and always has been, rehabilitation. The successes are not inconsiderable, the failures rather less than some of us imagine. Yet it is difficult in the extreme, with the poor amenities at our disposal, to apply social and particularly psychological therapy on the scale that makes any of it seem truly meaningful.

Brady, opting for solitary confinement on the extreme-security floor of Durham Prison, will be strongly urged to come out and make contact with other men: in fact, there is nothing to prevent him from opting for solitary confinement during the whole of his sentence. Some men, though a very few, have done so, and seem to have achieved a kind of contentment. There are natural solitaries outside our prisons, who seem to be happy enough making cells for themselves. It is likely that he will eventually be removed to a jail that makes provision for a free and more or less safe association between a certain category of prisoners.

As Sybille Bedford has put it, this seems to be "the best we can do."

11 - The Question of Madness *

Were they mad?

Certainly not under the M'Naghten Rules, and no plea of diminished responsibility was entered—to the surprise of many pressmen who, in the week before the trial, were expecting this, and consequently expecting a change in the trial procedure.

Did they seem mad?

I do not believe that anyone who sat through the whole, or even a part of, the trial felt that they were. They had brought themselves under a remarkable degree of self-control, in circumstances which, in some people, might have been sufficient *per se* to induce insanity. They were a stony pair: yet both were alert to every moment of the trial, incessantly passing notes to their solicitors, and, when not giving evidence, seemed extraordinarily relaxed. Brady, in particular, spent hours in doodling, head cocked, on his blue pad.

I have hitherto believed that anyone who committed

* The following chapter is written with due respect to the professional criminologist and psychologist. It simply offers some ideas of my own.

103

murder was in a sense mad: there seems to be a fragile barrier between the desire and the performance which is, thank God, unexpectedly powerful: as if it were a microcrystalline barrier which is able to hold back enormous pressures. In this case, the pressures had been broken. Yet it was impossible to feel that Brady and Hindley had gone mad—simply that they had settled for iniquity.

Had settled for it: theirs was a corporate action, the fantasy mulled over hour after hour, week after week, suddenly—it must surely have been sudden?—turning into a practical possibility. Was it at that unguessable moment that the barrier broke?

I am sorry to be rhetorical. There is little to be done except to ask questions

My impression was, and it is not the one I expected to have, that neither Hindley nor Brady were mad in any sense that I can recognize—that is, not as individuals. They had, in fact, drifted into a kind of corporate wickedness and no doubt had dragged, or had hoped to drag, others into it.

But the word "corporate" arouses its special problems, to which I shall return.

Consider a few notable murder cases.

Ruth Ellis was mad with jealousy when she shot her lover.

I cannot believe at all in the "madness" of Christopher Craig, or the luckless Bentley. This was a jaunt with a gun, and guns get fired.

Christie was driven mad by the mania of necrophilia, which is unusual, to say the least of it.

John George Haigh was driven "mad" by his mania for petty gain, in its turn aggravated by megalomania. I discount the bogus vampirism: I do not even believe he was a sadist. He was merely, as my grandmother would have put it, "too clever by half." The maddest thing about Haigh was his conviction that he could get away with it: he was a remarkably silly murderer.

Madeleine Smith might have been driven "mad" with fear at the possibility of public exposure by the turkeycock lover she had ceased to love: this, however, I doubt. She was an abnormally resolute young woman.

George Joseph Smith, with his side-manias for baths and harmoniums, seems to me as mad as it is given a man to be.

These may seem to be arbitrary distinctions, and are certainly within the realm of dispute: but for the purposes of this book, I think it is worth while to make them.

Unless we believe that it is mad to take life in any circumstances—which is just a tautology—then some killers are clearly and demonstrably sane. Crippen, I should have thought, was a case in point, and so, we should all accept, are many mercy killers.

Murder "madness," if I may use that word with very strict reservations, seems to occur in three distinct forms.

1. The "madness" induced in one person, venting itself on one person: through jealousy (Ruth Ellis, Bywaters), through fear of exposure (Madeleine Smith), through the desire to get an unpleasing or unloved person out of the way (Mahon, Crippen, Adelaide Bartlett, Mrs. Maybrick—though I have to say that in the case of the two women I feel their guilt is just open to reasonable doubt), through pure greed (Seddon).

2. The "madness" which induces multiple murder, through an unbridled form of perversion, directed by one person towards a number of persons: here we may have

greed *plus* some form of sexual perversion (George Joseph Smith), or greed plus a degree of megalomania (Vacquier, John George Haigh, Landru), or perversion for its own sake (Christie, Neville Heath, Fritz Harmann, Jack the Ripper).

3. Corporate murder by two or more people of one person (Leopold and Loeb, the Indianapolis case).

Affectlessness, in the Indianapolis trial, reached an appalling pitch *:

> Judy Duke, 12, one of several neighborhood small fry who witnessed the battering game, said that she had told her mother, "They are beating Sylvia something awful," adding, "My mother didn't do anything because she thought Sylvia was beaten for being bad." Mrs. Phyllis Vermillion, who lived next door and once heard the dying Sylvia scraping a shovel on the basement floor to attract aid, testified that the girl "looked like she didn't care whether she lived or died"—but said nothing about having helped her.

In the State of Indiana, all accused, the mother and the children, were liable to the death penalty. In fact, Mrs. Banizewski was convicted of murder and given a life-sentence: her daughter Paula, 18, of second-degree murder which carries a mandatory life-term, the three boys of manslaughter, which means from 2 to 21 years in prison. The only child in Mrs. Banizewski's dreadful family who told the prosecution all she knew is still awaiting trial.

Three court psychiatrists found the mother sane, so the insanity plea fell to the ground. "One conceded that she possessed 'a capacity for violent action,' which may have been aroused by Sylvia's calling her daughter Stepha-

* *Time* magazine, May 27, 1966.

nie, 15, a whore. As for the child sadists, it seemed that Mrs. Banizewski's blood-lust had infected them, and that Sylvia's passivity only whetted their murderous zeal."

I should consider Mrs. Banizewski quite mad, if only that she had deliberately initiated the most revolting cruelty in her children and her children's friends. Let me, however, return to my categories.

4. The "madness" which it is most difficult to understand: the corporate murder, by two or more people of two or more people. This is rare in the nineteenth and twentieth centuries, but was not so uncommon in the coven activities of the Middle Ages. The Moors Murder is a conspicuous example of this, and leads us to examine the crucial point: can madness be corporate?

I except from all claim to madness the gang killings in the United States in the 1920s and subsequent gang killings, in our country and others, from the Mafia downwards. This is not madness: it is violence motivated by greed or revenge and, I think, the lust for sheer organizational power. It is impossible to believe that all these historic gangsters, from Al Capone onwards, were mad in any clinical sense: this makes nonsense of the general concept that *all* killers are off their heads, a concept I myself held dear for many years and am now forced to abandon. (My concept that all suicides were mad was halted abruptly when Kruger, the Swedish "match king," killed himself. Obviously he preferred death to the long, unluxurious life in jail. Perhaps, in his situation, I might have made the same choice myself.)

However, let us look at the corporate killing, with more than one victim, in this way. In the corporation there is always, at first, a leader, a man or woman of *charisma*, who exerts power over weaker personalities.

Having got a second person into his power, he may fire a
power in them, thus creating another dangerous person
besides himself to continue with the work of corrupting
others. So it may go on, till the leaders of any "coven
group," as it were, become multiple powers over a much
larger, and sheeplike, majority.

Here in this present case we have to deal, and must
deal, with two persons only, since we have no evidence of
any wider involvement.

Let us presume that Brady is an aggressive psycho-
path, in the sense we use the term, though it is one we use
very loosely. He was certainly the dominant partner over
Hindley whom, as I have said before, seemed to have de-
rived from him power of her own. If the condition of this
couple is madness at all, it would seem to be a case of *folie
à deux,* and to approximate most nearly to the case of the
lesbic Papin sisters, cook and housemaid in Le Mans to
Madame and Mademoiselle Lancelin, who, in 1933, murdered their employers in circumstances of Gothic atrocity.
But they, unlike Brady and Hindley, saw themselves as
punishers—hadn't the victims scrawled "dirt" in the dust
on top of the bureau? They had this rationale, like the Indianapolis murderers, for what they did.

Brady and Hindley were punishing nobody; they were
simply acting out their desires, for pure self-gratification.
In their case, it begins to seem increasingly likely that they
were affected by what they read.

And I suggest that the flood of sadistic pornography
which is making the western world look so hideous (and,
incidentally, so absurd) was conducive to such "madness"
as may have been in them, and is conducive to a madness of
our whole society. Whether I am right or wrong, it is criminal and anti-social folly to refuse to examine the question.

12 - The Unreason
of the Clerks

There has, since the Moors Case acted as a catalyst, been a wave of disquiet among liberal-minded persons in England and America. Have we been acting on false assumptions? Have we been trying to identify with youth at all costs? Have we, in trying to be benevolent, been unrealistic?

For several years past, there has been an increasing demand that all things should be made available to all people, even to the suggestion that there should be no restriction on the sale of narcotics, or of hallucinatory drugs. The idea that the immature might need some protection from a mature society has been steadily battened down, chiefly on the grounds that the young "mature" more rapidly than they did twenty years ago. If maturation in this case means an earlier coming to puberty, it may be true: but only vestigially so. There has not, so far as one can tell, been any dramatic change in the age of menstruation since the end of World War II, though there has been a lowering of that age over a century. But if maturation in the physical sense were round about the age of eleven, this would not mean that the children were any more mature emotionally than before, and it is with the emotional aspect of growing up that we should be concerning ourselves, always remembering that emotional maturity is to a degree bound up with education, whether this latter is achieved by formal means or through the influence of an open-minded family background.

The Moors Case, far more repulsive in detail than most people have even begun to realize, did not seem to me an isolated incident, but like a septic wound that had burst in the entire body of our society. Out of our violence has sprung, also, the murder of the eight nurses in Chicago, the massacre by the sniper on the tower at Austin, Texas. The fact that some actions are performed by people who are mentally unbalanced does not mean that they cease to spring out of the pressures of a society.

There was some discussion in the Sunday papers, immediately after the verdict, as to how far an increasingly permissive society had contributed to what was done to Evans and the two children: but this provoked small public response, and there has been no subsequent impulse, so far as I can tell, to put a brake on the flow of sado-masochistic pornography as a whole.

The argument against restriction usually takes the same course. If we try to check any conceivable freedom of expression, won't that bring Hitlerism back? Isn't any kind of restriction bad in itself? Yet the whole history of social reform has been one of limited restriction of someone or something. Samuel Plimsoll, who came in for the most astonishing flood of abuse when he fought for a scheme that would prevent the overloading of ships and the drowning of sailors, was certainly attempting to restrict the freedom of certain ship owners to make money by taking the risks of shipwreck. The English Street Offences Act resulted in loss of a great deal of liberty for the pimp.

Is it not more socially dangerous to make, without a considerable period for reflection, all forms of reading and dramatic presentation available to everyone, than to study carefully those things which may *conceivably* be morally corrupting? A great deal of the material which the totally permissive intellectual would fight to preserve is devoted to an *alluring* recall to memory of the brutalities of the concentration camps.

Dr. George Steiner writes,* and I shall quote him again at some length:

> Our civilisation has recently produced and experienced a nightmare which is endurable only by virtue of careful forgetting. Everywhere around us inhumanity threatens or makes its philosophic aesthetic claims. Man, to the believer a fragment of God's image, to the agnostic an infinitely complex, precarious sum of natural forces, is very much in question. Will the wide dissemination of erotica and pornography, a major part of it firmly based on Sadism, add to the sum of emotional and humane literacy in our crowded community?

Some intellectuals, disputing this, are doing so out of benevolent motives I have mentioned earlier. Some are doing so either from vanity ("It's all right for me—*I'm* not affected") or from fear of being seen to swim against the tide.

Recently, I gave a talk to the literary society of a new university. My theme was broad—"On Writing Novels"— and much of it was by its nature personal. However, I then raised wider questions. Had "total permissiveness" made things easier, or harder, for the professional writer? I had seen an honorable American novelist of right-wing inclinations, unappreciated for years, make his first great suc-

* *The Times Literary Supplement,* June 25, 1966.

cess by putting in the Compulsory Sex Scene. It did not suit him. It made him look like a respectable gent who, in a passionate desire to be "with it," had adopted a pop singer's coiffure.

Had "total permissiveness" brought us a finer literature? If it had, I should like to know where to look for it.

Then I went further. Could total permissiveness result in a moral deterioration of a large section of society? I did not push the point much beyond enquiry.

Question time came. There were many questions: nearly all of them concerned with how I wrote, how I found my themes, what came first—character, theme or plot?—etc. Hardly one question was raised on the moral issues which had caused so notable a susurration while I was speaking.

In the bar afterwards, things were very different. Four or five students came to talk and drink with me, to ask me questions: and these questions, almost without exception, were directed to the moral issues I had raised. They were straightforward, searching and serious. But why were they only raised now? Had these excellent and thoughtful undergraduates been intimidated by popular pressures? Why had they been afraid to challenge my ideas, agree or disagree with them, merely *discuss* them, in public? Had they been seriously overborne by the presence of two or three young men who managed to protest against me by various forms of mime? This I cannot believe. But then, what am I to believe when I see this dichotomy between public and private expression? Surely, if the young get cold feet, it is a poor lookout for the rest of us.

It is very easy for anyone protesting, as I am, that we should stop right now and consider just what we are doing, to get very cold feet indeed. The response is almost invariably abuse of a strangely excitable nature: it is rarely sober and rational argument. Sometimes I find myself smiling on the wrong side of my face when I see praised as "courageous" some new novel seeking to make its mark by the almost incessant depiction of genital operations. It doesn't take courage any more either to do this or to boost it: it never takes courage merely to sing in chorus.

Our Clerks, however unreasoning, must know the basic reason for the deluge of sado-masochistic, "hard-core" pornography. This is not published by good, altruistic persons who believe they are helping to make a sweeter and more educated society. These may exist: but I have referred earlier to another force in a commercial society, which is an infinitely powerful one. People are publishing the stuff because there is money in it. The motive is, quite simply, profit, and this is the way they can make a quick, sure turnover.

The public is there. The early school-leaver, in his dead-end job, is earning far more than was even conceivable so little as twenty years ago. Blood is hot, experience still either fumbling or negligible. Not unnaturally he wants to "know," and there is an element of pathos in the fact that some boys and girls, spending out money for dirty and worthless books, are doing so not wholly out of lubriciousness, but out of a faint feeling that these may improve their education for living. The trouble is that they are entirely without instinct for selection, and unfitted by their meager schooling to take a serious work of sexology, for instance, in the spirit in which it was written. (I am not sure that most of us are, however we have been trained.) Every intellectual who believes this a valuable part of education might pause to consider whose pockets these young people are lining. Money: *merde*. While we are encouraging the total freedom of literary excreta, we ought not to forget the analogy.

I find it hard to understand the source of the guilty silence. For one brave voice like Dr. Steiner's, one can hear the constricted breathing of a hundred determined to be mute: it is like the breathing of the sea. I can well understand the impulse of many middle-aged people not to cut themselves off from the world of the young: an artificial barrier has already been erected between them and ourselves, and because of our loves and our anxieties we long to bridge it. Many childless people will automatically approve many adolescent demands, however ridiculous or pernicious these may be, because they have a special interest in keeping young and feel they can do so only by strenuous youth-identification. One must have some sympathy for this impulse, in its humanity and loneliness.

I am, however, obliged to believe that many intellectuals clamoring for total license have not really thought about the implications of what they are saying. Again, I quote Dr. Steiner's letter * in reply to Mr. Girodias.

> "Total freedom" of publication includes Streicher on the need to castrate all Jews; or any flysheet instructing us of the racial inferiority and sexual aggressiveness of Negroes or West Indians. If Mr. Girodias is in favour of such publications, let him say so.

I have never heard a single intellectual, when arguing his case for "total freedom," express that case in any but sexual terms. Yet "total" means what it says. I have never heard any one of them attempt to draw a line of any sort, or even to suggest that one might be drawn. If he did so, his whole case would fall to the ground: and he knows it.

* *The Times Literary Supplement,* May 26, 1966.

He is really thinking *only* in terms of a specific kind of permissiveness, but once he admitted this he would be in trouble. Would he, in fact, be prepared to tolerate the railway bookstall making a handsome show of Streicher on castration? If not, why not? I am quite sure it would sell.

To revert to the Moors Trial:

> Dr. Steiner: "What do we know about the literary aspects of the case (and by *we* I simply mean the general public)? The prosecution let it be known that it would make no more extensive reference to pornographic material in Brady's possession than was strictly necessary to obtain conviction. A work of Sade's was specifically mentioned as well as a serious study of him; *other* pornographic books having reference to erotic torture, flagellation and so forth were alluded to in the preliminaries of the trial. How many there were, and of what kind has not been disclosed."

(Since this letter was written, much of that book list has leaked out.)

> What has emerged, though again with little detail and in a way that allows no more than careful conjecture, is the high probability that the reading of Sade and related material was a significant factor in Brady's relations with Hindley. It would appear that the introduction of sadistic literature and certain types of pornography into a mind not previously familiar with the stuff *—to the semi-literate print conveys a peculiar authority, a power to neutralize or supersede personal consciousness—can contribute to the total disorientation of "normal" emotional habits and co-ordinates. Such disorientation may account for the willingness of a young woman to stand by

* The majority of Brady's books were of fairly recent paperback publication. (P.H.J.)

while a small girl is sexually humiliated and tormented. This potential of sadistic erotica to bewilder those who do not have counter-currents of wit, intellectual detachment, literary recognition, and to bewilder them in a way that creates a pathological consensus in two or more human beings *together* is precisely one of the possibilities I pointed to in my debate with Mr. Girodias.

Here many of our intellectuals profess to doubt (1) whether Brady and Hindley would not have done as they did even if they had read nothing but *Cranford*, (2) whether, if we draw a line at some things, we may not be forced into total restrictiveness.

Yet I have not heard any serious protest against the phrase "hard-core" pornography, of the kind seized by the police, so I must presume that the idea of a hard and soft core (whatever these may mean) is tacitly accepted. But surely to accept it means to acknowledge that some distinction *is* possible between strictly commercial filth, and the obscene book written by an artist? (This is not to say that very good artists may not also be pornographers.)

Perhaps I may make this tentative suggestion. Conceivably we should worry less about actual subject matter than the way in which the subject is treated. Consider the scene, in *A la recherche du temps perdu*, where M. de Charlus, in Jupien's male brothel, has himself chained to a bedstead and thrashed. There are writers who could only make this disgusting, and nothing more. How has Proust made it not only tolerable, but also funny and sad? He has done it by the device of irony: he himself gives not the slightest sign of being lubriciously involved.

Poor Charlus has so exhausted all other pleasures that only this one is left: and even this fails him, since it is a rotten fake, a dismal fraud.

After his session with the flogger, the Baron is bitterly disappointed.

> "I did not want to speak before that little fellow. He's very nice and does his best but he's not brutal enough. His face pleases me but he calls me a low debauchee as though he had learned it by heart." "Oh, dear no! No one has said a word to him," Jupien answered, without realising the unlikelihood of the assertion. "As a matter of fact, he was mixed up in the murder of a concierge in La Villette." "Indeed? that is rather interesting," said the Baron with a smile. "But I've just secured a butcher, a slaughterer, who looks rather like him; by a bit of luck he happened to look in. Would you like to try him?" "Yes, with pleasure."

The whole of this scene is deprived of corrupting force by the insistence that it *is* a fraud, the whole thing, and a shabby one. It is perhaps the supreme example of Proust's literary tact.

Professor Harry Levin, writing on "The Unbanning of the Books," professes considerable disquiet, though he is more hopeful of the outcome than I:

> If we abandon censorship, we depend all the more imperatively upon criticism. If we agree that books are neither dirty nor clean, we must be sure to remember that they are bad or good, and must not be distracted into ignoring that difference. After all, it has never been too difficult to tell a potboiler from a work of art, and it should be even simpler with potboilers that concentrate upon sex to the point of monotony. To criticise them is to discriminate between artistic imagination and autistic fantasy. One of the wholesome results of our hard-won candour is that it could end by driving the pornographers out of the business.

Greatly as I admire and respect Professor Levin, I feel that here he is touching no more than the fringe of the problem. Criticism rarely has to deal with any work not originally between hard covers, which means, in effect, with anything that does not even pretend to the condition of art. Critics are beginning to deal with bad pornography disguised as art, and some of that, certainly, may eventually be driven out. But only specialized, even journalistic, criticism has ever dealt with the scientific or pseudo-scientific work that has become a staple diet to the pornography-hound: one does not see long, serious reviews devoted to, say, *Orgies of Torture and Brutality.* Nor does criticism touch the plain rubbish of the *Pleasures of the Whip* or *Virgins of Shame* variety, which gushes onto the shelves with the tide that carried *Naked Lunch.*

Even while I have been writing this book, two ideas have hardened in my mind. The first is that we should concentrate on the study of *treatment* in the literary arts, rather than upon subject itself. Is there anything new under the sun? The other day, a young poet was deploring the fact that nobody had yet dealt with bestiality—forgetting, I am afraid, Ovid's *Metamorphoses.* Any subject is proper material for art—at least, I think so, though I would not be dogmatic even about this. People pondering on the theme may find certain ideas coming into their minds which are demonstrably absurd. However, let it go for the moment. Any subject—we can say, for the purposes of argument—is fit material for art: but we have to ask ourselves for what motive a certain subject was chosen, and to what effect was the treatment designed.

The second is that if we cannot reduce those seventy-five tons of pornography, then we should make them far less easy to get at. The egalitarian cry will arise:

"Is it better for you to read these things than it is for
the educationally underprivileged youth or girl?" *

Yes, it is better for me to read these things. I have become mithridated to most books through a lifetime of
reading: they haven't. But I know perfectly well that if I
read nothing else but pornography (Hindley and Brady did
read almost nothing else) I should be harmed spiritually
and intellectually. Therefore, I do not want to leave the
way wide open to something that is harmful—making wild
libertarian gestures while I do it—to the unprotected.

I fail to see why I should exploit such good fortune as
I have had to do social harm. It is the attitude of the New
Clerks that seems to me, at worst, self-righteous and, at
best, so thoughtless.

* I went to a grammar school, left at sixteen, and afterwards tried
to catch up with my education on my own.

13 - *The Imitative Factor*

In 1963, a totally serious war-film was shown in England. It was called *The Victors,* and the most moving and terrifying scene was the execution of a deserter after a court martial. Blindfolded, tied to a post, he awaited death by a firing squad, while, as an ironical comment, the audience heard background music from *Meet Me in St. Louis,* with Judy Garland singing, "Have Yourself a Merry Little Christmas."

I wonder whether Brady and Hindley saw it, or merely read about it, and whether it could have inspired them to the artistic touches by which they completed the tape-recording of the murder of Lesley Ann Downey? (This film had a general release on October 25, 1964, and could have been seen in Manchester, though it was not shown in Hyde, Cheshire, till January 17, 1965, after Lesley Ann's death. Here, of course, I am merely speculating as to whether it could have come the murderers' way.)

It is clear that two depraved people might have found a new inspiration for depravity in a serious and admirable work of art; this does not mean, I need hardly say, that such works of art should be banned. I do feel, however, that my suggestion leads us into the problem of imitation.

It was the French criminologist Gabriel Tarde (1843–1904) who first codified Three Laws of Imitation, which in essence are still thought to be valid by such modern experts as Dr. Hermann Mannheim.

The first law is that men in crowds or big cities tend to imitate one another in proportion to the closeness of their contact. This Tarde called "fashion." He held that in stable groups, whether in families or in the countryside, imitation is less and suffers from less mutation. "Fashion spreads a certain action, which eventually becomes rooted as a custom: but custom is subsequently uprooted by a new fashion which in its turn becomes a custom." *

The second law treats of the direction in which imitations are spread. As a rule, the superior is imitated by the inferior. From the history of crime, Tarde traced crimes such as "vagabondage, drunkenness, murder, death by poisoning." He suggested that these were at first the sole prerogative of royalty (I find his list of crimes, especially vagabondage, curious in a royal context) but that they seeped down through the population until in the latter part of the nineteenth century they were to be found at every social level. Indecent assault on children was found at first only in the great cities, but later spread beyond them. "Fashions" such as dismembering corpses began in Paris in 1876 and vitriol-throwing first occurred in 1895. Both "fashions" rapidly spread to other areas of France.

The third law he called the "law of insertion." "When two mutually exclusive fashions come together, one can be substituted for the other. When this happens,

* *Pioneers in Criminology*, edited by Hermann Mannheim (Stevens & Sons Ltd., 1960), essay by Margaret S. Wilson Vine.

there is a decline in the older method and an increase in the newer method. An example of this would be murder by knifing and murder by the gun. Tarde found that the former method had decreased while the latter had increased."

In Tarde's opinion, crime, like any social phenomenon, started as a fashion and became a custom. He was, for his time, a very liberal penologist, treating crime as a phenomenon which was social (i.e., arising from social conglomeration) and at the time anti-social. To him it was an industry, but a negative one.

Fashion.

What were the fashions which attracted Brady and Hindley? They were set not by the lower strata of society, but by the upper ones. It was those upper intellectual strata—novelists, playwrights, stage and film directors—who, fascinated by the violence of their imagined picture of the *lumpen* proletariat, turned that violence into a vogue, who made chic the whole paraphernalia of petty perversion, who made easily available and socially acceptable such writers as Sade, whose work had previously been more or less confined to specialist readership. Every one of us engaged in publication of any sort has to do an immense amount of self-searching.

Sade was simply not worth disinterring from the "reserved," or "special," shelves if this was to result in the corruption of minds unprepared or untrained to take a long, cool look at him. As I say, even Mr. Girodias is prepared to admit that, as an artist, he is no great shakes—certainly no major shakes if one may use such a phrase. Why, then, has he been touted around with such a fanfare of trumpets?

We mustn't be soft-baked. Let us not forget the money.

Some of Sade's most enthusiastic backers in the past

have hardly been of the sort most given to long, cool looks. Swinburne, for example—"Our prophet, our preacher, our poet" (great word-spinners are not necessarily sensible or responsible men): Pétrus Borel, self-styled the "Werewolf"—*"Une des gloires de la France,"* he said, of Sade, *"un martyr":* Baudelaire, a very great poet, but scarcely a man given to social reflection, who described him as *"l'homme naturel"* (God help us all). His supporters also include Blake, who believed Sade was jailed purely for his prophetic writings, Sainte-Beuve, Paulhan, and of course Guillaume Apollinaire: *"L'esprit le plus libre qui ait encore existé."*

Sade: a liberator, in fact, of the spirit. We know of two spirits, at least, whom he has liberated.

If it is admitted that crime and perversion are imitative, surely the trend-setters ought to be careful what trends they set. It is not without significance that the mere phrase "for kicks," which is totally affectless, caught on like the burning fox-brush through the stubble. The "kick" could mean anything, from pleasure at the contrived "happening" (a "happening" becomes by its nature nonsense if it has to be contrived) to the exertions of young thugs who beat up, blind or murder some old woman, some Negro, some tramp in Central Park.

The mere fact that people demand "kicks" means that they demand personal assuagement of the desire for pure sensation, no matter who gets hurt. I should be astonished if, to many young people, the word "kinky" had any perverse connotation at all, though if it has not, God only knows what they think the word means.

Between the wars one could buy on many bookstalls a magazine called *London Life,** which was devoted entirely to the fancier perversions. (I have always thought

* No relation whatsoever to the present publication.

the whole thing was written by a single, world-weary but ingenious old gentleman in a dingy back room.) There were articles by barbers, lovingly describing their emotions as they cropped off tresses three feet long: by nieces whose adored aunts tight-laced them or stuffed them into velvet exclusively: by mothers who had found some new way of humiliating their children: by men who loved to be saddled and ridden by chesty blondes: by girls who rejoiced in wrestling in mud: by youths who made appointments with other youths who wore mackintoshes: by transvestites as fervent in the proselytizing of their kinkiness as John Knox of his own brand of theology. It was a nauseous little production, and the fact that it was never (so far as I know) seized can only have been due to the innocence of the Public Prosecutor, who only seemed concerned, at that time, as to whether paintings of women included the pubic hair.

Now we are flooded out with literature that is an extension of the subject-matter contained in the pre-war *London Life*. Many of the clubs and bookshops of Soho are a spectacle which, so far as I have seen or read, no town has provided until now.

As I have said before, all this merely provides a kind of sardonic amusement to people who know about this kind of thing and can shrug it off. But do they never think what the effect of it may be upon people hitherto innocent? Do they imagine fantasies thereby induced are never put into practice? If so, they are even more naïf than I already supposed them to be.

Of course the question must recur: Brady had a record of animal-torture and a police record also. If he had not been exposed to any of our contemporary social dandruff, would things have gone with him otherwise? *It is pos-*

sible, and so long as it is possible we are in no position to turn our backs upon the obvious implications. Our instincts are always to shrug off the possible, while interesting ourselves solely in the probable. But we can't create a human society simply on the basis of statistical probability. I believe the Moors Trial has deprived us of the right to do it.

The history of one crime induced by reading about another is endless. Yet I would not, for this reason, suggest that crime should not be reported. A free press is a safeguard of society. The responsibility here falls on the proprietors and editors of the newspapers, to see that crime is reported as decently as possible, and in no more obscene detail than is necessary for a working comprehension of the evidence, and the facts relevant to the charge itself. The feeling that this had to be so, in the Moors Case, was so strong that it was, almost by common consent, translated into action.

There is a profound difference between crime reporting and the disseminating of sado-masochistic literature. In the one case, we are told simply what has been done: in the second, it is being suggested to us, even urged upon us, what we might do. And some of us do it. That is the point at issue.

Cruelty, like crime, is imitative. The words of certain pop songs are sickening in their lack of affect, and can only produce callousness in human relations—moreover, in the relations between young men and women who are in the greatest need of sensitive treatment. Occasionally a gasp does go up, as when Lenny Bruce made his repugnant joke about the Leopold and Loeb case—"Bobby Herman always was a snotty-nosed kid." Affectlessness used for the sake of stimulating affect? You might say so, though visceral repulsion greeted it none the less. However, the point at which we feel obliged to register protest is a bizarrely high one, and when such jokes as these have been forgotten, we are found waiting affably for the next flood of the same variety.

14 - For Better, for Worse?

After the First World War, William Healy and Cyril Burt replaced the idea of the "theory of imitation" by the idea of the "safety valve," or healthy outlet: and their ideas have been almost totally dominant in the thinking of literary intellectuals almost to this day. But child psychiatrists such as Lucien Bovet then raised their voices in protest at the idea that what was seen, for example, on the cinema screen could not imbue children with a false sense of values and perhaps influence them in later life, by means of a delayed action. Statistics of thirty years ago and more did not present an encouraging picture. Hermann Mannheim in *Comparative Criminology* writes:

> Statisticians and sociologists have analysed the contents of films and also compared the interest shown by delinquents and non-delinquents in the movies and television. It was found, for example, that out of 500 motion pictures analysed in the years 1920, 1925 and 1930 about 25–30 per cent had crime as their major theme and also that delinquents exhibited a far greater interest in the movies and went to the cinema far more often than non-

delinquents. With regard to the first, the film industry replied that, as crime played such a dominant role in our society, they as faithful and impartial recorders of modern life had the moral and social duty to give it its proper share in the contents of the movies. To this it might be retorted that if it should be found that boredom, hanging about and doing nothing was an important feature of society—as they actually are—the film-makers would be most reluctant to give them their true share as doing so might be bad business. It is similar with the time-worn argument that here as so often it is doubtful which came first, the wish or its alleged fulfilment.

Dr. Mannheim here writes with his usual cutting edge. What he says is, of course, related to my argument that directors of plays who want absolute license to produce all the truths of contemporary life might be unlikely to show enthusiasm for a play that showed brute hunger, physical hunger, hunger for bread: and nothing else.

Hilde Himmelweit, whose Nuffield Foundation study has opened a new perspective of thought, is reported as stating that psychological tests show that scenes of violence on television have no therapeutic effect, despite any moral tagged on at the end. Well, we have suspected those moral tags for a long time.

The professional psychologists appear to be turning away more and more from the comforting and infinitely permissive theory of catharsis: a word long contorted out of its original meaning, just as some of our "cathartic" plays, films and television offerings would have caused some raised eyebrows from the unflinching but discreet playwrights of ancient Greece.

It is claimed by Professor Sprott and others that there is little crime in China, especially recidivist crime, and

very little juvenile delinquency, because of the moral
fervor which infects the entire community and of the
weight of public opinion upon the individual. We may
feel, as indeed I do, that the weight of such "moral fervor"
might be intolerable for us to bear, that our individualism
is such that we do not want public opinion breathing
down our necks: public opinion can be a very unpleasant
and meddlesome thing, and we in western society have become rich enough to keep it in its place. But the facts are
not in doubt.

When the Sermon on the Mount was bundled into
the dustbin (or, indeed, any code of ideas that had raised
men's eyes from the ground) a moral vacuum was created:
and the liberal humanists have not succeeded in filling it.
What was destroyed in one kind of society was any real
sense of human purpose—which includes social purpose.

People deeply need purpose, and to say to them, "It is
sufficient that you behave in the interests of society as a
whole," is simply not enough. It is far too abstract an ap-
proach to be any sort of guide to decent living. The Com-
munists found their faith in building a new society from
scratch. It will be splendid for them, splendid, and safer,
for us all, when the greater part of that building is com-
plete, when the stimulus of back-breaking endeavor has
gone, and they can live the cushioned life that we do in the
west. But I suspect that when that day comes, they will dis-
cover a moral vacuum, all right. Even now, many young
people in the Soviet Union are giving trouble because they
feel purpose has departed from them.

This is the paradox presenting itself when any achieve-
ment, from the building of a real socialist society to the
building of a welfare state, comes to some sort of fruition,
so far as the majority is concerned. It is a fearful question,

and one to which we must somehow find an answer if we are not to see the bright day, for which we longed, for which we worked, darken into blackest disappointment.

The error of the liberal humanists is that they have been unable to offer an alternative faith to the one they have renounced, except for faith in the beneficial effects of total permissiveness in every form of culture. This faith is a romantic one, even more romantic than Rousseau's. Once they ceased to believe even in the possibility of sheer iniquity and replaced this by a belief in Freud, they tore up the very stones of self-discipline and moral responsibility.

Mr. Hooson, counsel for Brady, read to David Smith an excerpt from Sade: " 'God is a disease, a plague, a weight round a man's neck.' " He asked whether those were Smith's own views.

Smith: "Oh, God, yes."

Here again, from a corrupted boy, is the easy *assumption* that Christianity is no longer believed in by anybody at all. What goes for Smith, must go for all.

It seems obvious that a country with a powerful social purpose is going to have a lower crime-rate than one which has not. Yet we cannot create social purpose artificially.

It is also idealistic to think that the comfortable society can, on a great scale—and great scales are necessary—turn its social purpose to the relief of societies less fortunate than themselves. Czechoslovakia was "a faraway country of which we know nothing," according to Neville Chamberlain. Yet it is much nearer to us than Africa. A great deal is being done for famine relief and the like: but public fervor cannot be snagged where public imagination is at a low ebb. To be told that millions of people are hungry may move us intellectually: but since we have never been, in their sense, hungry, we do not know what it means. To see a photograph of a starving child is not to see a starving child, many starving children: starvation has a *smell,* and this we cannot conceive.

The concept of *finding* social purpose may make us despair. But despair is a rottenness: it is so theologically, it is so socially. Because we cannot easily find answers, that is no excuse for not continuing to seek them out. Without social purpose, life becomes a bore, however cushioned, however easeful, however baroque a bore: and boredom certainly breeds crime, or excites the demand for sensation which is the prime supplier of new ideas for anti-social behavior.

15 - Under the Carpet

I asked a far-sighted friend of mine: "Do you suppose, now it is demonstrated that a young man and woman may have played out the fantasies of dirty books in murdering a youth and two children, people will look around and wonder whether the total-permissive craze towards violence and sexual cruelty oughtn't just possibly to be checked?"

He replied gloomily, "Not a bit of it. They will try to sweep it all under the carpet and as quickly as they damned well can."

The first attempt appeared in *The Daily Mail,* on Friday May 13, a distraction by the raising of side issues.

The writer first took the attorney-general to task for himself undertaking the prosecution. " . . . If the Attorney-General imagines that murder by shooting or stabbing is somehow less wicked than murder by poisoning or in the course of sadistic practices, or that the murder of an adult is less wicked than that of a child, he ought to have his moral judgment examined."

All this seems to me distinctly rum. I feel that there are degrees in murder, though these were recognized most unsatisfactorily in the Homicide Act of 1957. To me the murder of a child, or anyone else, in the course of sadistic practices (though the deaths of Lesley Ann Downey and John Kilbride were not incidental to those practices but climactic, since neither child could have been allowed to go free to tell the tale) is certainly more wicked than, say, the shooting of her lover by a woman crazed with jealousy, such as Ruth Ellis. Murder by slow poisoning is more wicked than murder in a fit of rage, or in a frenzy to escape capture (see Gunther Podola), and anyone who cannot see a distinction appears to me to be devoid of moral insight.

We need not, of course, make false apologies: murder is always wicked.

The writer continues to attack Sir Elwyn Jones for not leading the prosecution, personally, in the case of the Train Robbers. "For if ever there was a crime against good order and lawfulness it was that one—*far more so than any murder*—essentially (except perhaps in gang-killing cases) a personal matter, involving society only obliquely."

I have already expressed my distaste for the public deification of the Train Robbers who beat up the guard and left him a permanent invalid. But the contention that this crime was a more serious matter for society than the murders by Hindley and Brady seems to me the raising of property rights above individual human rights to the nth degree.

The article goes on: "The worst thing about the whole business is the deep hypocrisy in the British attitude to murder which claims that no madman may be punished and at the same time insists that the madder the murderer, the more heavily he should in fact be punished. . . . Can anyone seriously dispute—to throw the stone back into the center of the pool, where it belongs—that if the word 'mad' had any meaning at all, Myra Hindley and Ian Brady were mad?"

I do dispute this, and so would any of the observers to whom I talked during my spell in Chester. Nobody who was present felt them to be so, in any meaningful sense. They were no more mad than the S.S. guards at Auschwitz, and there were *hundreds* of the latter: when we begin to think about sado-masochistic behavior which results in murder, by people in the mass, then we have to stop using the word "mad" as an easy stereotype, and consider afresh what we mean by it.

It must be the natural desire of anyone who read through the evidence in the Moors Case, who was present at the trial, to clean it right out of the mind. It has degraded us all, it has soiled our imaginations. Yet we dare forget it no more than we dare forget Belsen or Auschwitz, unless we are trying to prove—as people *are* trying to prove—that the Moors Case was an isolated incident, having no springs in our society. Nobody, I think, has cared to say the same about the Nazi murderers.

In a personal letter to myself, Dr. George Steiner writes: "I hope you will say that the Trial was no surprise to those who have eyes to see and hearts to feel."

It can have come as no surprise at all to anyone watching the phenomena arising out of, alas, our Affluent Society. We could have smelled the stench of those corpses while they were still unburied.

Pearl Binder * wrote: "It [the case] is almost like a Computer . . . you feed in all the conditions and you get just all the crime to be expected. I found the affluent-society symbols (car, transistor set, tapes, wine, cameras)

* Lady Elwyn Jones, personal letter.

made it all an especial horror. And in all this the pornographic books must have played their part."

The more I reflect, the more I believe they did. Certainly it is preposterous—and evil—to make any ready
assumption that they did not.

But what has also played its part is a society with a
mania for *sensation*.* We are all getting now like M. de
Charlus, who, having exhausted his usual pleasures, got
more and more frantic in his desire to find new ones—and
found that, in this field as in every other, there was nothing new under the sun. We are equally frenzied in our desire to make the perversions acceptable, from the sadistic
maiming and killing, to flagellation, transvestism—
anything you like to name.

These things are not being forced upwards through
society because they are mass-desired: they are being forced
down through the unreason of the New Clerks, who tend to
turn away their heads when they find that perversion in
the name of "art" becomes transmuted, the further down
it seeps into our world, into a horrible, Coney Island vul-
garity of the spirit.

Shortly after the war, a vigorous campaign was waged
to stop horror-comics entering this country to corrupt our
children, and for a while it was successful. Nowadays it is
even hard to arouse enough public enthusiasm for a move
to stop the influx of American bubble-gum, the packets
containing pictures of a revoltingly sadistic nature. Don't
we care? Perhaps our children are not of the kind who buy
bubble-gum. Then have we no concern for the children
who do buy it? I suspect that here, as in other cases, we are
being smug, intellectually arrogant—or ourselves affectless.

* William Cooper, *The Listener*, June 9, 1966.

I cannot be sure about Brady, but I cannot help feeling that Hindley, had she lived in a different society, might not have done these things. In that sense, because we don't seem to care what ugliness we are disseminating, we *are* responsible for what has happened: but not each of us as an individual. We are only responsible if we have noticed what is going on around us, and have turned our eyes away.

As I have said, with the Moors Case, the wound of our world broke open, we looked into it, and we smelled its sepsis. It is, to me, the purest self-deception to pretend that our Ugly Society played no part whatsoever in what happened on the housing estate at Hattersley, Cheshire. Of course it did.

I am not, and again I emphasize this, suggesting easy solutions: in fact, I am suggesting none. I am only suggesting, as straightforwardly as I can, that we have a lot of rethinking to do. If once we become afraid to think, then we are lost, and we are for anyone's picking.

It all comes back to Ivan Karamazov. What price would we pay to prevent the torturing of one helpless child? The price of restricting art? I don't answer this question. I simply ask it.

16 - Romantic Agonies

It might have been better for me, as an individual, if I had had nothing to do with this case at all.

It has left a mark which I think will never quite be eradicated. People who talk about the trial, who have followed, even closely, the press reports, have small idea what it actually meant: what actually happened. What did happen to Lesley Ann Downey, as is generally agreed by those close to the case, I cannot put on paper. I cannot even let the "facts" turn to realities in the forefront of my mind.

We may think, with excitement, about vice: how many of us know what it is? Between the pleasant idea and the reality is the gauze. It sets us apart from what is real, as a proscenium stage sets us apart from the play.

The idea of vice is something most of us domesticate. It *is* all a play, isn't it? The ideas of Sade may stimulate us —but would *we* attempt to practice them? To us it is a game. To the accused in the dock at Chester it was not a game.

"People don't do such things." Oh, but they do. We are, most of us, play actors: what we do is in fun. The

thought of what we might do moistens the spirit. But would we do it, in actuality? Of course not. That is why we feel so safe. We are still in the front row of the dress-circle.

To write of vice, of cruelty, without having any actual confrontation with either, is the purest frivolity. "Who's for tennis?" It is as frivolous as that, but it is harmful. Who ever really bounced through that mythical french window, waving a racket? Who ever tortured, maimed or killed, and was free to write about the process?

Blame the press, if you like, for encouraging as much ignorance as was humanly possible in the Moors Case. (I don't.) But we must not pose, in the arts, as comprehenders of cruelty, violence, sadism, if we have never come into real, as opposed to intellectual, contact with any of these things. If we do so, we are no more than buskers.

The genuine artist can only speak of what he knows innately—or of what he actually knows. All else is romanticization. I am not asking anyone wholly to abandon the theory that, for all sins, environment and the behavior of mother or father are responsible, though I think we have carried it much too far, and laid upon many helpless parents a burden of guilt they find it hard to carry. Much of our thinking in this respect is little more than metaphor. I am asking him to consider whether some actions, which I should, and do, call wicked, may not have some relevance to a genetic factor: or, going further, whether it may be quite impossible for us, on the evidence provided, to see those actions in terms of iniquity?

There is always a dividing line between what we feel we want to do, and what we *do* do. That line presents a profound mystery. Brady and Hindley, discussing the murder of a child for kicks—well, I know nobody who would discuss such a thing. But we must assume that they were

people as excited by such discussions as others are by LSD.
At some point, this pair crossed the line.

"Madam"—said the attorney-general, for once height-
ening a word in a sardonic sense—"a child, of your own
sex?"

Hindley shot her pale-blue cuffs and she frowned a
little. Then her face returned to its customary impassivity.

All right, she was incapable of realizing fully what she
had done. But any intellectual who propounds cruelty for
the sake of "kicks," and does know what he is doing, is socially frivolous.

It is not enough for us to suggest, as most of us would,
that man has made of this world a horrible place, hold up
the mirror, and leave it at that. We can still make of our
world what we will: if we *"will"* in a positive direction. To
sit on our haunches and bewail the mess we have made,
without considering how we might contrive to get out of
that mess, is frivolity carried a million light-years beyond
the frivolity of an old Aldwych farce. The Theater of
Cruelty is a black frivolity of which we may some day be
ashamed.

Unlike Ivan Karamazov, I have not returned God his
ticket. Had I meant to do that, I should have done so after
seeing the dreadful film of the overrunning of Belsen:
with those shaven, mindless men and women in the uni-
form of clowns, tottering about the bone-littered com-
pounds amidst the strewn squalor of death. It is from a
derivation of all this that we are now attempting to make
the stuff of art.

After the first day of the trial, I went into a Chester
bookshop to find something to read, something that would
take my mind off what I had heard, that should be as far as
humanly possible from it. I bought a Wodehouse novel,

and a classical detective story by a woman writer whom I had always admired.* I found it quite impossible to read either. Both were too far removed from reality as I had seen it that day. One was a fairy-tale; one was patently absurd, in the terms of what murder is like. For days I could not read an entertainment novel without seeing the faces of Hindley and Brady imprinting themselves upon the page.

In a review of Louis-Ferdinand Céline, Mr. Anthony Burgess writes, with his usual brilliant fireworks-display of imagery:

> A world in which everybody is both torturer and victim has the nasty vitality of a head of hair ridden with fleas, but it is better than bourgeois death.

Surely it is not. This is the height of Romantic Agony thinking, and implies the usual rhetorician's failure to distinguish between real death and death as a metaphor. The "world in which everybody is both torturer and victim" is the Nazi world that leads to real death. What does Mr. Burgess actually mean by "bourgeois death?" A vegetable family, well fed, in a neat little house with plastics everywhere, perpetually watching the telly, while the children stuff iced lollies and Mum's hand is always reaching out for another chocolate? A depressing picture, certainly. But it is a picture of a situation where, each in his own way, everybody is content, nobody is tortured, nobody gets killed.

* It is rubbish for Mr. Girodias to equate the effect of the classical crime novel with that of the pornographic. In the former, the problem is all that matters: the best work in this genre is deliberately unsensational, so far as the "murder" goes. This kind of novel is certainly getting swamped by the thick-ear, Private Eye, semi-pornographic school: but Mrs. Christie, for example, is not in the same category as Mr. Mickey Spillane, and there is no point in pretending that she is.

Don't we tend to look at the way of "bourgeois death" from what is really a snobbish angle? Don't we feel so intellectually superior to these vegetables of our imagining, so infinitely more free, more vital, that we want to destroy them, wreck their peace, stone their windows, smash up their telly? They would not be at all grateful to us for releasing them from what we believe to be their parlous state, and we shall never, never, I fear, get them to see how very much better and more full of life is a head of hair crawling with lice than one which has just had a Beauty Kreme shampoo.

Fancified cruelty, I have just suggested, is a sin: and so, I have also suggested, is fancified despair. I have met many writers who have written most eloquently and hopelessly about their own despair and the world's: they have, almost to a man, turned out to be the most prosperous and comfortable of beings. There is a danger, an almost insuperable temptation, that we in advanced societies tend to put on expressions of agonized seriousness and then to play at things.

I recognize that our position is not easy. It is not easy largely for reasons that we do not want to recognize. Many of the grosser problems in our country, in America, all round the richer part of the world, have been solved. Most of us, whatever our protestations, do not want to interfere with the situation we have inherited: and so, at the edge, we play with sensations, with a metaphysical despair. We do not want to recognize that our situation is not remotely the same as that of most of our fellow human beings: we play at things, we enjoy the kicks, while they go hungry. In a comparable historical context, Sade and the *penseurs* whom we are so anxious to revive did just the same.

I recognize that it is difficult not to swim with the

tide. Some of those vigorously pushing with the tide cannot pretend that their motives are disinterested: publishers of pornographic literature, producers of plays of sensation, writers of the works so published and produced, depend both for reputation and crude money on the ultimate irresponsible tide. Nevertheless, there are many who genuinely are disinterested, such as Mr. Anthony Burgess, whom I have quoted with respect. But I believe that many good people, so gentle that they would not listen to one second of Brady's tape-recording, so anxious to spread enlightenment, have not yet realized to what extent they are children of their time.

We are all children of our time. But nearly anything worth doing is done against the tide. This has been so in all societies and is now. We need now to begin to look again at the extravagant subjectivism which began to be our climate a couple of generations ago. We need to think much less about what we are capable of fancying, and much more about how we act. We need to think of our own behavior: and our own behavior includes what we say and write.

Behavior—in our subjectivism, we have sometimes forgotten this—is the test of what we can make of ourselves and others. Yes, we are all sinful. The hope is that we can behave as though we were a shade better than that. We are all capable of dreaming of iniquity: the hope is that we can avoid committing it. It is iniquity, of course, to encourage by any means iniquity in others. How can we live our lives so as to make the behavior of Hindley and of Brady just a shade less likely?